W9-CHP-227

DATE DUE

Wind, Sand and Stars

By the author of
NIGHT FLIGHT

Illustrated by

John O'H. Cosgrave, II

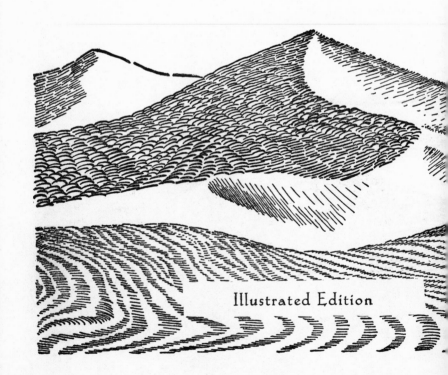

Illustrated Edition

Wind, Sand and Stars

by

Antoine de Saint Exupéry

Translated from the French by

Lewis Galantière

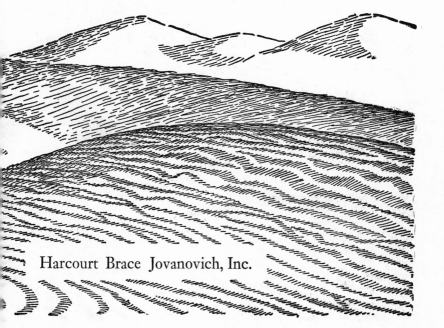

Harcourt Brace Jovanovich, Inc.

T.6.70
ISBN 0-15-197085-8

9650

A French Aviator who followed the profession of Airline Pilot for Eight Years offers the American edition of this book in homage to the Airline Pilots of America and their Dead

Contents

· 1 ·

The Craft

IN 1926 I was enrolled as student airline pilot by the Latécoère Company, the predecessors of Aéropostale (now Air France) in the operation of the line between Toulouse, in southwestern France, and Dakar, in French West Africa. I was learning the craft, undergoing an apprenticeship served by all young pilots before they were allowed to carry the mails. We took ships up on trial spins, made meek little hops between Toulouse and Perpignan, and had dreary lessons in meteorology in a freezing hangar. We lived in fear of the mountains of Spain, over which we had yet to fly, and in awe of our elders.

These veterans were to be seen in the field restaurant—gruff, not particularly approachable, and inclined somewhat to condescension when giving us the benefit of their experience. When one of them landed, rain-soaked and behind schedule, from Alicante or Casablanca, and one of us asked humble questions about his flight, the very curtness of his replies on these tempestuous days was matter enough out of which to build a fabulous world filled with snares and pitfalls, with cliffs suddenly looming out of fog and whirling air-currents of a strength to uproot cedars. Black dragons guarded the mouths of the valleys and clusters of lightning crowned the crests—for our elders were always at some pains to feed our reverence. But from time to time one or another of them, eternally to be revered, would fail to come back.

I remember, once, a homecoming of Bury, he who was later to die in a spur of the Pyrenees. He came into the restaurant, sat down at the common table, and went stolidly at his food, shoulders still bowed by the fatigue of his recent trial. It was at the end of one of those foul days when from end to end of the line the skies are filled with dirty weather, when the mountains seem to a pilot to be wallowing in slime like exploded cannon on the decks of an antique man-o'-war.

I stared at Bury, swallowed my saliva, and ventured after a bit to ask if he had had a hard flight. Bury, bent over his plate in frowning absorption, could not hear me. In those days we flew open ships and thrust our heads out round the windshield, in bad weather, to take our bearings: the wind that whistled in our ears was a long time clearing out of our heads. Finally Bury looked up, seemed to understand me, to think back to what I was referring to, and suddenly he gave a bright laugh. This brief burst of laughter, from a man who laughed little, startled me. For a moment his weary being was bright with it. But he spoke no word, lowered his head, and went on chewing in silence. And in that dismal restaurant, surrounded by the simple government clerks who sat there repairing the wear and tear of their humble daily tasks, my broad-shouldered messmate seemed to me strangely noble; beneath his rough hide I could discern the angel who had vanquished the dragon.

The night came when it was my turn to be called to the field manager's room.

He said: "You leave tomorrow."

I stood motionless, waiting for him to dismiss me. After a moment of silence he added:

"I take it you know the regulations?"

In those days the motor was not what it is today. It would drop out, for example, without warning and with a great rattle like the crash of crockery. And one would simply throw in one's hand: there was no hope of refuge on the rocky crust of Spain. "Here," we used to say, "when your motor goes, your ship goes, too."

An airplane, of course, can be replaced. Still, the important thing was to avoid a collision with the range; and blind flying through a sea of clouds in the mountain zones was subject to the severest penalties. A pilot in trouble who buried himself in the white cotton-wool of the clouds might all unseeing run straight into a peak. This was why, that night, the deliberate voice repeated insistently its warning:

"Navigating by the compass in a sea of clouds over Spain is all very well, it is very dashing, but—"

And I was struck by the graphic image:

"But you want to remember that below the sea of clouds lies eternity."

And suddenly that tranquil cloud-world, that world so harmless and simple that one sees below on rising out of the clouds, took on in my eyes a new quality. That peaceful world became a pitfall. I imagined the immense white pitfall spread beneath me. Below it reigned not what one might think—not the agitation of men, not the living tumult and bustle of cities, but a silence even more absolute than in the clouds, a peace even more final. This viscous whiteness became in my mind the frontier between the real and the unreal, between the known and the unknowable. Already I was beginning to realize that a spectacle has no meaning except it be seen through the glass of a culture, a civilization, a craft. Mountaineers too know the sea of clouds.

yet it does not seem to them the fabulous curtain it is to me.

When I left that room I was filled with a childish pride. Now it was my turn to take on at dawn the responsibility of a cargo of passengers and the African mails. But at the same time I felt very meek. I felt myself ill-prepared for this responsibility. Spain was poor in emergency fields; we had no radio; and I was troubled lest when I got into difficulty I should not know where to hunt a landing-place. Staring at the aridity of my maps, I could see no help in them; and so, with a heart full of shyness and pride, I fled to spend this night of vigil with my friend Guillaumet. Guillaumet had been over the route before me. He knew all the dodges by which one got hold of the keys to Spain. I should have to be initiated by Guillaumet.

When I walked in he looked up and smiled.

"I know all about it," he said. "How do you feel?"

He went to a cupboard and came back with glasses and a bottle of port, still smiling.

"We'll drink to it. Don't worry. It's easier than you think."

Guillaumet exuded confidence the way a lamp gives off light. He was himself later on to break the record for postal crossings in the Andes and the South Atlantic. On this night, sitting in his shirtsleeves, his arms folded in the lamplight, smiling the most heartening of smiles, he said to me simply:

"You'll be bothered from time to time by storms, fog, snow. When you are, think of those who went through it before you, and say to yourself, 'What they could do, I can do.'"

I spread out my maps and asked him hesitantly if he would mind going over the hop with me. And there, bent over in the lamplight, shoulder to shoulder with the veteran, I felt a sort of schoolboy peace.

But what a strange lesson in geography I was given! Guillaumet did not teach Spain to me, he made the country my friend. He did not talk about provinces, or peoples, or livestock. Instead of telling me about Guadix, he spoke of three orange-trees on the edge of the town: "Beware of those trees. Better mark them on the map." And those three orange-trees seemed to me thenceforth higher than the Sierra Nevada.

He did not talk about Lorca, but about a humble farm near Lorca, a living farm with its farmer and the farmer's wife. And this tiny, this remote couple, living a thousand miles from where we sat, took on a universal importance. Settled on the slope of a mountain, they watched like lighthouse-keepers beneath the stars, ever on the lookout to succor men.

The details that we drew up from oblivion, from their inconceivable remoteness, no geographer had been concerned to explore. Because it washed the banks of great cities, the Ebro River was of interest to mapmakers. But what had they to do with that brook running secretly through the water-weeds to the west of Motril, that brook nourishing a mere score or two of flowers?

"Careful of that brook: it breaks up the whole field. Mark it on your map." Ah, I was to remember that serpent in the grass near Motril! It looked like nothing at all, and its faint murmur sang to no more than a few frogs; but it slept with one eye open. Stretching its length along the grasses in the paradise of that emergency landing-field, it lay in wait for me a thousand miles from where I sat. Given the chance, it would transform me into a flaming candelabra. And those thirty valorous sheep ready to charge me on the slope of a hill! Now that I knew about them I could brace myself to meet them.

"You think the meadow empty, and suddenly bang! there are thirty sheep in your wheels." An astounded smile was all I could summon in the face of so cruel a threat.

Little by little, under the lamp, the Spain of my map became a sort of fairyland. The crosses I marked to indicate safety zones and traps were so many buoys and beacons. I charted the farmer, the thirty sheep, the brook. And, exactly where she stood, I set a buoy to mark the shepherdess forgotten by the geographers.

When I left Guillaumet on that freezing winter night, I felt the need of a brisk walk. I turned up my coat collar, and as I strode among the indifferent passers-by I was escorting a fervor as tender as if I had just fallen in love. To be brushing past these strangers with that marvelous secret in my heart filled me with pride. I seemed to myself a sentinel standing guard over a sleeping camp. These passers-by knew nothing about me, yet it was to me that, in their mail pouches, they were about to confide the weightiest cares of their hearts and their trade. Into my hands were they about to entrust their hopes. And I, muffled up in my cloak, walked among them like a shepherd, though they were unaware of my solicitude.

Nor were they receiving any of those messages now being despatched to me by the night. For this snowstorm that was gathering, and that was to burden my first flight, concerned my frail flesh, not theirs. What could they know of those stars that one by one were going out? I alone was in the confidence of the stars. To me alone news was being sent of the enemy's position before the hour of battle. My footfall rang in a universe that was not theirs.

These messages of such grave concern were reaching me as I walked between rows of lighted shop-windows, and those windows on that night seemed a display of all that was good on earth, of a paradise of sweet things. In the sight of all this happiness, I tasted the proud intoxication of renunciation. I was a warrior in danger. What meaning could they have for me, these flashing crystals meant for men's festivities, these lamps whose glow was to shelter men's meditations, these cozy furs out of which were to emerge pathetically beautiful solicitous faces? I was still wrapped in the aura of friendship, dazed a little like a child on Christmas Eve, expectant of surprise and palpitatingly prepared for happiness; and yet already I was soaked in spray; a mail pilot, I was already nibbling the bitter pulp of night flight.

It was three in the morning when they woke me. I thrust the shutters open with a dry snap, saw that rain was falling on the town, and got soberly into my harness. A half-hour later I was out on the pavement shining with rain, sitting on my little valise and waiting for the bus that was to pick me up. So many other flyers before me, on their day of ordination, had undergone this humble wait with beating heart.

Finally I saw the old-fashioned vehicle come round the corner and heard its tinny rattle. Like those who had gone before me, I squeezed in between a sleepy customs guard and a few glum government clerks. The bus smelled musty, smelled of the dust of government offices into which the life of a man sinks as into a quicksand. It stopped every five hundred yards to take on another scrivener, another guard, another inspector.

Those in the bus who had already gone back to sleep responded with a vague grunt to the greeting of the newcomer, while he crowded in as well as he was able and instantly fell asleep himself. We jolted mournfully over the uneven pavements of Toulouse, I in the midst of these men who in the rain and the breaking day were about to take up again their dreary diurnal tasks, their red tape, their monotonous lives.

Morning after morning, greeted by the growl of the customs guard shaken out of sleep by his arrival, by the gruff irritability of clerk or inspector, one mail pilot or another got into this bus and was for the moment indistinguishable from these bureaucrats. But as the street lamps moved by, as the field drew nearer and nearer, the old omnibus rattling along lost little by little its reality and became a grey chrysalis from which one emerged transfigured.

Morning after morning a flyer sat here and felt of a sudden, somewhere inside the vulnerable man subjected to his neighbor's surliness, the stirring of the pilot of the Spanish and African mails, the birth of him who, three hours later, was to confront in the lightnings the dragon of the mountains; and who, four hours afterwards, having vanquished it, would be free to decide between a détour over the sea and a direct assault upon the Alcoy range, would be free to deal with storm, with mountain, with ocean.

And thus every morning each pilot before me, in his time, had been lost in the anonymity of daybreak beneath the dismal winter sky of Toulouse, and each one, transfigured by this old omnibus, had felt the birth within him of the sovereign who, five hours later, leaving behind him the rains and snows of the North, repudiating winter, had throttled down his motor and begun to drift earthward in the summer air beneath the shining sun of Alicante.

The old omnibus has vanished, but its austerity, its discomfort, still live in my memory. It was a proper symbol of the apprenticeship we had to serve before we might possess the stern joys of our craft. Everything about it was intensely serious. I remember three years later, though hardly ten words were spoken, learning in that bus of the death of Lécrivain, one of those hundred pilots who on a day or a night of fog have retired for eternity.

It was four in the morning, and the same silence was abroad when we heard the field manager, invisible in the darkness, address the inspector:

"Lécrivain didn't land at Casablanca last night."

"Ah!" said the inspector. "Ah?"

Torn from his dream he made an effort to wake up, to display his zeal, and added:

"Is that so? Couldn't he get through? Did he come back?"

And in the dead darkness of the omnibus the answer came: "No."

We waited to hear the rest, but no word sounded. And as the seconds fell it became more and more evident that that "no" would be followed by no further word, was eternal and without appeal, that Lécrivain not only had not landed at Casablanca but would never again land anywhere.

And so, at daybreak on the morning of my first flight with the mails, I went through the sacred rites of the craft, and I felt the self-confidence oozing out of me as I stared through the windows at the macadam shining and reflecting back the street lights. Over the pools of water I could see great palms of wind running. And I thought: "My first flight with the mails! Really, this is not my lucky day."

I raised my eyes and looked at the inspector. "Would you call this bad weather?" I asked.

He threw a weary glance out of the window. "Doesn't prove anything," he growled finally.

And I wondered how one could tell bad weather. The night before, with a single smile Guillaumet had wiped out all the evil omens with which the veterans overwhelmed us, but they came back into my memory. "I feel sorry for the man who doesn't know the whole line pebble by pebble, if he runs into a snow-storm. Oh, yes, I pity the fellow." Our elders, who had their prestige to think of, had all bobbed their heads solemnly and looked at us with embarrassing sympathy, as if they were pitying a flock of condemned sheep.

For how many of us had this old omnibus served as

refuge in its day? Sixty? Eighty? I looked about me. Luminous points glowed in the darkness. Cigarettes punctuated the humble meditations of worn old clerks. How many of us had they escorted through the rain on a journey from which there was no coming back?

I heard them talking to one another in murmurs and whispers. They talked about illness, money, shabby domestic cares. Their talk painted the walls of the dismal prison in which these men had locked themselves up. And suddenly I had a vision of the face of destiny.

Old bureaucrat, my comrade, it is not you who are to blame. No one ever helped you to escape. You, like a termite, built your peace by blocking up with cement every chink and cranny through which the light might pierce. You rolled yourself up into a ball in your genteel security, in routine, in the stifling conventions of provincial life, raising a modest rampart against the winds and the tides and the stars. You have chosen not to be perturbed by great problems, having trouble enough to forget your own fate as man. You are not the dweller upon an errant planet and do not ask yourself questions to which there are no answers. You are a petty bourgeois of Toulouse. Nobody grasped you by the shoulder while there was still time. Now the clay of which you were shaped has dried and hardened, and naught in you will ever awaken the sleeping musician, the poet, the astronomer that possibly inhabited you in the beginning.

The squall has ceased to be a cause of my complaint.

The magic of the craft has opened for me a world in which I shall confront, within two hours, the black dragons and the crowned crests of a coma of blue lightnings, and when night has fallen I, delivered, shall read my course in the stars.

Thus I went through my professional baptism and I began to fly the mails. For the most part the flights were without incident. Like sea-divers, we sank peacefully into the depths of our element.

Flying, in general, seemed to us easy. When the skies are filled with black vapors, when fog and sand and sea are confounded in a brew in which they become indistinguishable, when gleaming flashes wheel treacherously in these skyey swamps, the pilot purges himself of the phantoms at a single stroke. He lights his lamps. He brings sanity into his house as into a lonely cottage on a fearsome heath. And the crew travel a sort of submarine route in a lighted chamber.

Pilot, mechanic, and radio operator are shut up in what might be a laboratory. They are obedient to the play of dial-hands, not to the unrolling of the landscape. Out of doors the mountains are immersed in tenebrous darkness; but they are no longer mountains, they are invisible powers whose approach must be computed.

The operator sits in the light of his lamp, dutifully setting down figures; the mechanic ticks off points on his chart; the pilot swerves in response to the drift of the mountains as quickly as he sees that the summits he intends to pass on the left have deployed straight ahead of him in a silence and secrecy as of military preparations. And below on the ground the watchful radio men in their shacks take down submissively in their notebooks the dictation of their comrade in the air: "12:40 a.m. En route 230. All well."

So the crew fly on with no thought that they are in motion. Like night over the sea, they are very far from the earth, from towns, from trees. The motors fill the lighted chamber with a quiver that changes its substance. The clock ticks on. The dials, the radio lamps, the various hands and needles go through their invisible alchemy. From second to second these mysterious stirrings, a few muffled words, a concentrated tenseness, contribute to the end result. And when the hour is at hand the pilot may glue his forehead to the window with perfect assurance. Out of oblivion the gold has been smelted: there it gleams in the lights of the airport.

And yet we have all known flights when of a sudden, each for himself, it has seemed to us that we have crossed the border of the world of reality; when, only a couple of hours from port, we have felt ourselves more distant from it than we should feel if we were in India; when there has come a premonition of an incursion into a forbidden world whence it was going to be infinitely difficult to return.

Thus, when Mermoz first crossed the South Atlantic in a hydroplane, as day was dying he ran foul of the Black Hole region, off Africa. Straight ahead of him were the tails of tornadoes rising minute by minute gradually higher, rising as a wall is built; and then the night came down upon these preliminaries and swallowed them up; and when, an hour later, he slipped under the clouds, he came out into a fantastic kingdom.

Great black waterspouts had reared themselves seemingly in the immobility of temple pillars. Swollen at their tops, they were supporting the squat and lowering arch of the tempest, but through the rifts in the arch there fell slabs of light and the full moon sent her radiant beams between the pillars down upon the frozen tiles of the sea. Through these uninhabited ruins Mermoz made his way, gliding slantwise from one channel of light to the next, circling round those giant pillars in which there must have rumbled the upsurge of the sea, flying for four hours through these corridors of moonlight toward the exit from the temple. And this spectacle was so overwhelming that only after he had got through the Black Hole did Mermoz awaken to the fact that he had not been afraid.

I remember, for my part, another of those hours in which a pilot finds suddenly that he has slipped beyond the confines of this world. All that night the radio messages sent from the ports in the Sahara concerning our position had been inaccurate, and my radio operator, Néri, and I had been drawn out of our course. Suddenly, seeing the gleam of water at the bottom of a crevasse of fog, I tacked sharply in the direction of the coast; but it was by then impossible for us to say how long we had been flying towards the high seas. Nor were we certain of making the coast, for our fuel was probably low. And even so, once we had reached it we would still have to make port—after the moon had set.

We had no means of angular orientation, were already deafened, and were bit by bit growing blind. The moon like a pallid ember began to go out in the banks of fog. Overhead the sky was filling with clouds, and we flew thenceforth between cloud and fog in a world voided of all substance and all light. The ports that signaled us had given up trying to tell us where we were. "No bearings, no bearings," was all their message, for our voice reached them from everywhere and nowhere. With sinking hearts Néri and I leaned out, he on his side and I on mine, to see if anything, anything at all, was distinguishable in this void. Already our tired eyes were seeing things—errant signs, delusive flashes, phantoms.

And suddenly, when already we were in despair, low on the horizon a brilliant point was unveiled on our port bow. A wave of joy went through me. Néri leaned forward, and I could hear him singing. It could not but be the beacon of an airport, for after dark the whole

Sahara goes black and forms a great dead expanse. That light twinkled for a space—and then went out! We had been steering for a star which was visible for a few minutes only, just before setting on the horizon between the layer of fog and the clouds.

Then other stars took up the game, and with a sort of dogged hope we set our course for each of them in turn. Each time that a light lingered a while, we performed the same crucial experiment. Néri would send his message to the airport at Cisneros: "Beacon in view. Put out your light and flash three times." And Cisneros would put out its beacon and flash three times while the hard light at which we gazed would not, incorruptible star, so much as wink. And despite our dwindling fuel we continued to nibble at the golden bait which each time seemed more surely the true light of a beacon, was each time a promise of a landing and of life—and we had each time to change our star.

And with that we knew ourselves to be lost in interplanetary space among a thousand inaccessible planets, we who sought only the one veritable planet, our own, that planet on which alone we should find our familiar countryside, the houses of our friends, our treasures.

On which alone we should find . . . Let me draw the picture that took shape before my eyes. It will seem to you childish; but even in the midst of danger a man retains his human concerns. I was thirsty and I was hungry. If we did find Cisneros we should re-fuel and carry on to Casablanca, and there we should come down in the cool of daybreak, free to idle the hours away. Néri and I would go into town. We would go to a little pub already open despite the early hour. Safe and sound, Néri and I would sit down at table and laugh at the night of danger as we ate our warm rolls and drank our bowls of coffee and hot milk. We would receive this matutinal gift at the hands of life. Even as an old peasant woman recognizes her God in a painted image, in a childish medal, in a chaplet, so life would speak to us in its humblest language in order that we understand. The joy of living, I say, was summed up for me in the remembered sensation of that first burning and aromatic swallow, that mixture of milk and coffee and bread by which men hold communion with tranquil pastures, exotic plantations, and golden harvests, communion with the earth. Amidst all these stars there was but one that could make itself significant for us by composing this aromatic bowl that was its daily gift at dawn. And from that earth of men, that earth docile to the reaping of grain and the harvesting of the grape, bearing its rivers asleep in their fields, its villages clinging to their hillsides, our ship was separated by astronomical distances. All the treasures of the world were summed up in a grain of dust now blown far out of our path by the very destiny itself of dust and of the orbs of night.

And Néri still prayed to the stars.

Suddenly he was pounding my shoulder. On the bit

of paper he held forth impatiently to me I read: "All well. Magnificent news." I waited with beating heart while he scribbled the half-dozen words that were to save us. At last he put this grace of heaven into my hands.

It was dated from Casablanca, which we had left the night before. Delayed in transmission, it had suddenly found us more than a thousand miles away, suspended between cloud and fog, lost at sea. It was sent by the government representative at the airport. And it said: "Monsieur de Saint Exupéry, I am obliged to recommend that you be disciplined at Paris for having flown too close to the hangars on leaving Casablanca."

It was true that I had done this. It was also true that this man was performing his duty with irritability. I should have been humiliated if this reproach had been addressed to me in an airport. But it reached me where it had no right to reach me. Among these too rare stars, on this bed of fog, in this menacing savor of the sea, it burst like a detonation. Here we were with our fate in our hands, the fate of the mails and of the ship; we had trouble enough to try to keep alive; and this man was purging his petty rancor against us.

But Néri and I were far from nettled. What we felt was a vast and sudden jubilation. Here it was we who were masters, and this man was letting us know it. The impudent little corporal! not to have looked at our stripes and seen that we had been promoted captain! To

intrude into our musings when we were solemnly taking our constitutional between Sagittarius and the Great
Bear! When the only thing we could be concerned with,
the only thing of our order of magnitude, was this
appointment we were missing with the moon!

The immediate duty, the only duty of the planet
whence this man's message came, was to furnish us ac-
curate figures for our computations among the stars.
And its figures had been false. This being so, the planet
had only to hold its tongue. Néri scribbled: "Instead of
wasting their time with this nonsense they would do
better to haul us back to Cisneros, if they can." By
"they" he meant all the peoples of the globe, with their
parliaments, their senates, their navies, their armies, their
emperors. We re-read the message from that man mad
enough to imagine that he had business with us, and
tacked in the direction of Mercury.

It was by the purest chance that we were saved. I had
given up all thought of making Cisneros and had set my
course at right angles to the coast-line in the hope that
thus we might avoid coming down at sea when our fuel
ran out. Meanwhile however I was in the belly of a
dense fog so that even with land below it was not going
to be easy to set the ship down. The situation was so
clear that already I was shrugging my shoulders ruefully
when Néri passed me a second message which, an hour
earlier, would have been our salvation. "Cisneros," it
said, "has deigned to communicate with us. Cisneros

says, '216 doubtful.'" Well, that helped. Cisneros was no longer swallowed up in space, it was actually out there on our left, almost within reach. But how far away? Néri and I talked it over briefly, decided it was too late to try for it (since that might mean missing the coast), and Néri replied: "Only one hour fuel left continuing on 93."

But the airports one by one had been waking each other up. Into our dialogue broke the voices of Agadir, Casablanca, Dakar. The radio stations at each of these towns had warned the airports and the ports had flashed the news to our comrades. Bit by bit they were gathering round us as round a sick-bed. Vain warmth, but human warmth after all. Helpless concern, but affectionate at any rate.

And suddenly into this conclave burst Toulouse, the headquarters of the Line three thousand miles away, worried along with the rest. Toulouse broke in without a word of greeting, simply to say sharply: "Your reserve tanks bigger than standard. You have two hours fuel left. Proceed to Cisneros."

There is no need of nights like the one just described to make the airline pilot find new meanings in old appearances. The scene that strikes the passenger as commonplace is from the very moment of taking off animated with a powerful magic for the crew. It is the duty of the ship's captain to make port, cost what it may. The sight of massing clouds is no mere spectacle to him: it is a matter of concern to his physical being, and to his mind it means a set of problems. Before he is off the ground he has taken its measure, and between him and it a bond is formed which is a veritable language.

There is a peak ahead, still distant. The pilot will not reach it before another hour of flight in the night. What is to be the significance of that peak? On a night of full moon it will be a useful landmark. In fainter moonglow it will be a bit of wreckage strewn in shadow, dangerous, but marked clearly enough by the lights of villages. But if the pilot flies blind, has bad luck in correcting his drift, is dubious about his position, that peak begins to stir with a strange life and its threat fills the breadth of the night sky in the same way as a single mine, drifting at the will of the current, can render the whole of the ocean a danger.

The face of the sea is as variable as that of the earth. To passengers, the storm is invisible. Seen from a great height, the waves have no relief and the packets of fog have no movement. The surface of the sea appears to be covered with great white motionless palm-trees, palms marked with ribs and seams stiff in a sort of frost. The sea is like a splintered mirror. But the hydroplane pilot knows there is no landing here.

The hours during which a man flies over this mirror are hours in which there is no assurance of the possession of anything in the world. These palms beneath the plane are so many poisoned flowers. And even when the flight is an easy one, made under a shining sun, the pilot navigating at some point on the line is not gazing upon a scene. These colors of earth and sky, these traces of wind over the face of the sea, these clouds golden in the afterglow, are not objects of the pilot's admiration, but of his cogitation. He looks to them to tell him the direction of the wind or the progress of the storm, and the quality of the night to come.

Even as the peasant strolling about his domain is able to foresee in a thousand signs the coming of the spring, the threat of frost, a promise of rain, so all that happens in the sky signals to the pilot the oncoming snow, the expectancy of fog, or the peace of a blessed night. The machine which at first blush seems a means of isolating man from the great problems of nature, actually plunges him more deeply into them. As for the peasant so for the pilot, dawn and twilight become events of consequence. His essential problems are set him by the mountain, the sea, the wind. Alone before the vast tribunal of the tempestuous sky, the pilot defends his mails and debates on terms of equality with those three elemental divinities.

The mail pouches for which he is responsible are stowed away in the after hold. They constitute the dogma of the religion of his craft, the torch which, in this aerial race, is passed from runner to runner. What matter though they hold but the scribblings of tradesmen and nondescript lovers. The interests which dictated them may very well not be worth the embrace of man and storm; but I know what they become once they have been entrusted to the crew, taken over, as the phrase is. The crew care not a rap for banker or trades-man. If, some day, the crew are hooked by a cliff it will not have been in the interest of tradespeople that they will have died, but in obedience to orders which ennoble the sacks of mail once they are on board ship.

What concerns us is not even the orders—it is the men they cast in their mould.

· 2 ·

The Men

MERMOZ is one airline pilot, and Guillaumet another, of whom I shall write briefly in order that you may see clearly what I mean when I say that in the mould of this new profession a new breed of men has been cast.

I

A handful of pilots, of whom Mermoz was one, surveyed the Casablanca-Dakar line across the territory inhabited by the refractory tribes of the Sahara. Motors in those days being what they were, Mermoz was taken prisoner one day by the Moors. The tribesmen were unable to make up their minds to kill him, kept him a captive a fortnight, and he was eventually ransomed. Whereupon he continued to fly over the same territory.

When the South American line was opened up Mermoz, ever the pioneer, was given the job of surveying the division between Buenos Aires and Santiago de Chile. He who had flung a bridge over the Sahara was now to do the same over the Andes. They had given him a plane whose absolute ceiling was sixteen thousand feet and had asked him to fly it over a mountain range that rose more than twenty thousand feet into the air. His job was to search for gaps in the Cordilleras. He who had studied the face of the sands was now to learn the contours of the peaks, those crags whose scarfs of snow flutter restlessly in the winds, whose surfaces are bleached white in the storms, whose blustering gusts sweep through the narrow walls of their rocky corridors and force the pilot to a sort of hand-to-hand combat. Mermoz enrolled in this war in complete ignorance of his adversary, with no notion at all of the chances of coming forth alive from battle with this enemy. His job was to "try out" for the rest of us. And, "trying out" one day, he found himself prisoner of the Andes.

Mermoz and his mechanic had been forced down at an altitude of twelve thousand feet on a table-land at whose edges the mountain dropped sheer on all sides.

For two mortal days they hunted a way off this plateau. But they were trapped. Everywhere the same sheer drop. And so they played their last card.

Themselves still in it, they sent the plane rolling and bouncing down an incline over the rocky ground until it reached the precipice, went off into air, and dropped. In falling, the plane picked up enough speed to respond to the controls. Mermoz was able to tilt its nose in the direction of a peak, sweep over the peak, and, while the water spurted through all the pipes burst by the night frost, the ship already disabled after only seven minutes of flight, he saw beneath him like a promised land the Chilean plain.

And the next day he was at it again.

When the Andes had been thoroughly explored and the technique of the crossings perfected, Mermoz turned over this section of the line to his friend Guillaumet and set out to explore the night. The lighting of our airports had not yet been worked out. Hovering in the pitch black night, Mermoz would land by the faint glimmer of three gasoline flares lined up at one end of the field. This trick, too, he taught us, and then, having tamed the night, he tried the ocean. He was the first, in 1931, to carry the mails in four days from Toulouse to Buenos Aires. On his way home he had engine trouble over a stormy sea in mid-Atlantic. A passing steamer picked him up with his mails and his crew.

Pioneering thus, Mermoz had cleared the desert, the

mountains, the night, and the sea. He had been forced down more than once in desert, in mountain, in night, and in sea. And each time that he got safely home, it was but to start out again. Finally, after a dozen years of service, having taken off from Dakar bound for Natal, he radioed briefly that he was cutting off his rear right-hand engine. Then silence.

There was nothing particularly disturbing in this news. Nevertheless, when ten minutes had gone by without report there began for every radio station on the South Atlantic line, from Paris to Buenos Aires, a period of anxious vigil. It would be ridiculous to worry over someone ten minutes late in our day-to-day exist-ence, but in the air-mail service ten minutes can be pregnant with meaning. At the heart of this dead slice of time an unknown event is locked up. Insignificant, it may be; a mishap, possibly: whatever it is, the event has taken place. Fate has pronounced a decision from which there is no appeal. An iron hand has guided a crew to a sea-landing that may have been safe and may have been disastrous. And long hours must go by before the de-cision of the gods is made known to those who wait.

We waited. We hoped. Like all men at some time in their lives we lived through that inordinate expectancy which like a fatal malady grows from minute to minute harder to bear. Even before the hour sounded, in our hearts many among us were already sitting up with the dead. All of us had the same vision before our eyes. It

was a vision of a cockpit still inhabited by living men;
but the pilot's hands were telling him very little now,
and the world in which he groped and fumbled was a
world he did not recognize. Behind him, in the glimmer
of the cabin light, a shapeless uneasiness floated. The
crew moved to and fro, discussed their plight, feigned
sleep. A restless slumber it was, like the stirring of
drowned men. The only element of sanity, of intelli-
gibility, was the whirring of the three engines with its
reassuring evidence that time still existed for them.

We were haunted for hours by this vision of a plane
in distress. But the hands of the clock were going round
and little by little it began to grow late. Slowly the truth
was borne in upon us that our comrades would never
return, that they were sleeping in that South Atlantic
whose skies they had so often ploughed. Mermoz had
done his job and slipped away to rest, like a gleaner who,
having carefully bound his sheaf, lies down in the field
to sleep.

When a pilot dies in the harness his death seems something that inheres in the craft itself, and in the beginning the hurt it brings is perhaps less than the pain
sprung of a different death. Assuredly he has vanished,
has undergone his ultimate mutation; but his presence
is still not missed as deeply as we might miss bread. For
in this craft we take it for granted that we shall meet
together only rarely.

Airline pilots are widely dispersed over the face of the world. They land alone at scattered and remote airports, isolated from each other rather in the manner of sentinels between whom no words can be spoken. It needs the accident of journeyings to bring together here or there the dispersed members of this great professional family.

Round the table in the evening, at Casablanca, at Dakar, at Buenos Aires, we take up conversations interrupted by years of silence, we resume friendships to the accompaniment of buried memories. And then we are off again.

Thus is the earth at once a desert and a paradise, rich in secret hidden gardens, gardens inaccessible, but to which the craft leads us ever back, one day or another. Life may scatter us and keep us apart; it may prevent us from thinking very often of one another; but we know that our comrades are somewhere "out there"—where, one can hardly say—silent, forgotten, but deeply faithful. And when our path crosses theirs, they greet us with such manifest joy, shake us so gaily by the shoulders! Indeed we are accustomed to waiting.

Bit by bit, nevertheless, it comes over us that we shall never again hear the laughter of our friend, that this one garden is forever locked against us. And at that moment begins our true mourning, which, though it may not be rending, is yet a little bitter. For nothing, in truth, can replace that companion. Old friends cannot be created out of hand. Nothing can match the treasure of common memories, of trials endured together, of quarrels and reconciliations and generous emotions. It is idle, having planted an acorn in the morning, to expect that afternoon to sit in the shade of the oak.

So life goes on. For years we plant the seed, we feel ourselves rich; and then come other years when time does its work and our plantation is made sparse and thin. One by one, our comrades slip away, deprive us of their shade.

This, then, is the moral taught us by Mermoz and his kind. We understand better, because of him, that what constitutes the dignity of a craft is that it creates a fellowship, that it binds men together and fashions for them a common language. For there is but one veritable problem—the problem of human relations.

We forget that there is no hope of joy except in human relations. If I summon up those memories that have left with me an enduring savor, if I draw up the balance sheet of the hours in my life that have truly counted, surely I find only those that no wealth could have procured me. True riches cannot be bought. One cannot buy the friendship of a Mermoz, of a companion to whom one is bound forever by ordeals suffered in common. There is no buying the night flight with its hundred thousand stars, its serenity, its few hours of sovereignty. It is not money that can procure for us that new vision of the world won through hardship—those trees, flowers, women, those treasures made fresh by the dew and color of life which the dawn restores to us, this concert of little things that sustain us and constitute our compensation.

Nor that night we lived through in the land of the unconquered tribes of the Sahara, which now floats into my memory.

Three crews of Aéropostale men had come down at the fall of day on the Rio de Oro coast in a part of the Sahara whose denizens acknowledge no European rule. Riguelle had landed first, with a broken connecting rod. Bourgat had come along to pick up Riguelle's crew, but a minor accident had nailed him to earth. Finally, as night was beginning to fall, I arrived. We decided to salvage Bourgat's ship, but we should have to spend the night and do the job of repair by daylight.

Exactly on this spot two of our comrades, Gourp and Erable, had been murdered by the tribesmen a year earlier. We knew that a raiding party of three hundred rifles was at this very moment encamped somewhere near by, round Cape Bojador. Our three landings had been visible from a great distance and the Moors must have seen us. We began a vigil which might turn out to be our last.

Altogether, there were about ten of us, pilots and mechanics, when we made ready for the night. We unloaded five or six wooden cases of merchandise out of the hold, emptied them, and set them about in a circle. At the deep end of each case, as in a sentry-box, we set a lighted candle, its flame poorly sheltered from the wind. So in the heart of the desert, on the naked rind of the planet, in an isolation like that of the beginnings of the world, we built a village of men.

Sitting in the flickering light of the candles on this kerchief of sand, on this village square, we waited in the night. We were waiting for the rescuing dawn—or for the Moors. Something, I know not what, lent this night a savor of Christmas. We told stories, we joked, we sang songs. In the air there was that slight fever that reigns over a gaily prepared feast. And yet we were infinitely poor. Wind, sand, and stars. The austerity of Trappists. But on this badly lighted cloth, a handful of men who possessed nothing in the world but their memories were sharing invisible riches.

We had met at last. Men travel side by side for years, each locked up in his own silence or exchanging those words which carry no freight—till danger comes. Then they stand shoulder to shoulder. They discover that they belong to the same family. They wax and bloom in the recognition of fellow beings. They look at one another and smile. They are like the prisoner set free who marvels at the immensity of the sea.

Happiness! It is useless to seek it elsewhere than in this warmth of human relations. Our sordid interests imprison us within their walls. Only a comrade can grasp us by the hand and haul us free.

And these human relations must be created. One must go through an apprenticeship to learn the job. Games and risk are a help here. When we exchange manly handshakes, compete in races, join together to save one of us who is in trouble, cry aloud for help in the hour of danger—only then do we learn that we are not alone on earth.

Each man must look to himself to teach him the meaning of life. It is not something discovered: it is something moulded. These prison walls that this age of trade has built up round us, we can break down. We can still run free, call to our comrades, and marvel to hear once more, in response to our call, the pathetic chant of the human voice.

II

Guillaumet, old friend, of you too I shall say a few words. Be sure that I shall not make you squirm with any clumsy vaunting of your courage and your professional valor. In telling the story of the most marvelous of your adventures, I am after something quite different.

There exists a quality which is nameless. It may be gravity, but the word does not satisfy me, for the quality I have in mind can be accompanied by the most cheerful gaiety. It is the quality of the carpenter face to face

with his block of wood. He handles it, he takes its measure. Far from treating it frivolously, he summons all
his professional virtues to do it honor.

I once read, Guillaumet, a tale in which your adventure was celebrated. I have an old score to settle with the
infidel who wrote it. You were described as abounding
in the witty sallies of the street arab, as if courage consisted in demeaning oneself to schoolboy banter in the
midst of danger and the hour of death. The man did not
know you, Guillaumet. You never felt the need of
cheapening your adversaries before confronting them.
When you saw a foul storm you said to yourself, "Here
is a foul storm." You accepted it, and you took its
measure.

These pages, Guillaumet, written out of my memory,
are addressed in homage to you.

It was winter and you had been gone a week over the
Andes. I had come up from farthest Patagonia to join
Deley at Mendoza. For five days the two of us, each in
his plane, had ransacked the mountains unavailingly.
Two ships! It seemed to us that a hundred squadrons
navigating for a hundred years would not have been
enough to explore that endless, cloud-piercing range.
We had lost all hope. The very smugglers themselves,
bandits who would commit a crime for a five-peso note,
refused to form a rescue party out of fear of those coun-

terforts. "We should surely die," they said; "the Andes never give up a man in winter."

And when Deley and I landed at Santiago, the Chilean officers also advised us to give you up. "It is midwinter," they said; "even if your comrade survived the landing, he cannot have survived the night. Night in those passes changes a man into ice."

And when, a second time, I slipped between the towering walls and giant pillars of the Andes, it seemed to me I was no longer seeking, but was now sitting up with your body in the silence of a cathedral of snow.

You had been gone a week, I say, and I was lunching between flights in a restaurant in Mendoza when a man stuck his head in the door and called out:

"They've found Guillaumet!"

All the strangers in the restaurant embraced.

Ten minutes later I was off the ground, carrying two mechanics, Lefebvre and Abri. Forty minutes later I had landed alongside a road, having recognized from the air, I know not by what sign, the car in which you were being brought down from San Rafael. I remember that we cried like fools; we put our arms about a living Guillaumet, resuscitated, the author of his own miracle. And it was at that moment that you pronounced your first intelligible sentence, a speech admirable in its human pride:

"I swear that what I went through, no animal would have gone through."

Later, you told us the story. A storm that brought fifteen feet of snow in forty-eight hours down on the Chilean slope had bottled up all space and sent every other mail pilot back to his starting point. You, however, had taken off in the hope of finding a rift in the sky. You found this rift, this trap, a little to the south, and now, at twenty thousand feet, the ceiling of clouds being a couple of thousand feet below you and pierced by only the highest peaks, you set your course for Argentina.

Down currents sometimes fill pilots with a strange uneasiness. The engines run on, but the ship seems to be sinking. You jockey to hold your altitude: the ship loses speed and goes mushy. And still you sink. So you give it up, afraid that you may have jockeyed too much; and you let yourself drift to right or left, striving to put at your back a favorable peak, that is, a peak off which the winds rebound as off a springboard.

And yet you go on sinking. The whole sky seems to be coming down on you. You begin to feel like the victim of some cosmic accident. You cannot land anywhere, and you try in vain to turn round and fly back into those zones where the air, as dense and solid as a pillar, had held you up. That pillar has melted away. Everything here is rotten and you slither about in a sort of universal decomposition while the cloud-bank rises apathetically, reaches your level, and swallows you up.

"It almost had me in a corner once," you explained,

"but I still wasn't sure I was caught. When you get up above the clouds you run into those down currents that seem to be perfectly stationary for the simple reason that in that very high altitude they never stop flowing. Everything is queer in the upper range."

And what clouds!

"As soon as I felt I was caught I dropped the controls and grabbed my seat for fear of being flung out of the ship. The jolts were so terrible that my leather harness cut my shoulders and was ready to snap. And what with the frosting on the panes, my artificial horizon was invisible and the wind rolled me over and over like a hat in a road from eighteen thousand feet down to ten.

"At ten thousand I caught a glimpse of a dark horizontal blot that helped me right the ship. It was a lake, and I recognized it as what they call Laguna Diamante. I remembered that it lay at the bottom of a funnel, and that one flank of the funnel, a volcano called Maipu, ran up to about twenty thousand feet.

"There I was, safe out of the clouds; but I was still blinded by the thick whirling snow and I had to hang on to my lake if I wasn't to crash into one of the sides of the funnel. So down I went, and I flew round and round the lake, about a hundred and fifty feet above it, until I ran out of fuel. After two hours of this, I set the ship down on the snow—and over on her nose she went.

"When I dragged myself clear of her I stood up. The wind knocked me down. I stood up again. Over I went a second time. So I crawled under the cockpit and dug me out a shelter in the snow. I pulled a lot of mail sacks round me, and there I lay for two days and two nights. Then the storm blew over and I started to walk my way out. I walked for five days and four nights."

But what was there left of you, Guillaumet? We had found you again, true; but burnt to a crisp, but shriveled, but shrunken into an old woman. That same afternoon I flew you back to Mendoza, and there the cool white sheets flowed like a balm down the length of your body.

They were not enough, though. Your own foundered body was an encumbrance: you turned and twisted in your sleep, unable to find lodgment for it. I stared at your face: it was splotched and swollen, like an over-ripe fruit that has been repeatedly dropped on the ground.

You were dreadful to see, and you were in misery, for you had lost the beautiful tools of your work: your hands were numb and useless, and when you sat up on the edge of your bed to draw a free breath, your frozen feet hung down like two dead weights. You had not even finished your long walk back, you were still panting; and when you turned and stirred on the pillow in search of peace, a procession of images that you could not escape, a procession waiting impatiently in the wings, moved instantly into action under your skull. Across the stage of your skull it moved, and for the

twentieth time you fought once more the battle against
these enemies that rose up out of their ashes.

I filled you with herb-teas.

"Drink, old fellow."

"You know . . . what amazed me . . ."

Boxer victorious, but punch-drunk and scarred with
blows, you were re-living your strange adventure. You
could divest yourself of it only in scraps. And as you
told your dark tale, I could see you trudging without
ice-axe, without ropes, without provisions, scaling cols
fifteen thousand feet in the air, crawling on the faces of
vertical walls, your hands and feet and knees bleeding in
a temperature twenty degrees below zero.

Voided bit by bit of your blood, your strength, your
reason, you went forward with the obstinacy of an ant,
retracing your steps to go round an obstacle, picking
yourself up after each fall to earth, climbing slopes that
led to abysses, ceaselessly in motion and never asleep, for
had you slept, from that bed of snow you would never
have risen. When your foot slipped and you went
down, you were up again in an instant, else had you
been turned into stone. The cold was petrifying you by
the minute, and the price you paid for taking a moment
too much of rest, when you fell, was the agony of re-
vivifying dead muscles in your struggle to rise to your
feet.

You resisted temptation. "Amid snow," you told me,
"a man loses his instinct of self-preservation. After two

or three or four days of tramping, all you think about is sleep. I would long for it; but then I would say to myself, 'If my wife still believes I am alive, she must believe that I am on my feet. The boys all think I am on my feet. They have faith in me. And I am a skunk if I don't go on.' "

So you tramped on; and each day you cut out a bit more of the opening of your shoes so that your swelling and freezing feet might have room in them.

You confided to me this strange thing:

"As early as the second day, you know, the hardest job I had was to force myself not to think. The pain was too much, and I was really up against it too hard. I had to forget that, or I shouldn't have had the heart to go on walking. But I didn't seem able to control my mind. It kept working like a turbine. Still, I could more or less choose what I was to think about. I tried to stick to some film I'd seen, or book I'd read. But the film and the book would go through my mind like lightning. And I'd be back where I was, in the snow. It never failed. So I would think about other things. . . ."

There was one time, however, when, having slipped, and finding yourself stretched flat on your face in the snow, you threw in your hand. You were like a boxer emptied of all passion by a single blow, lying and listening to the seconds drop one by one into a distant universe, until the tenth second fell and there was no appeal.

"I've done my best and I can't make it. Why go on?"

All that you had to do in the world to find peace was to shut your eyes. So little was needed to blot out that world of crags and ice and snow. Let drop those miraculous eyelids and there was an end of blows, of stumbling falls, of torn muscles and burning ice, of that burden of life you were dragging along like a worn-out ox, a weight heavier than any wain or cart.

Already you were beginning to taste the relief of this snow that had now become an insidious poison, this morphia that was filling you with beatitude. Life crept out of your extremities and fled to collect round your heart while something gentle and precious snuggled in close at the centre of your being. Little by little your consciousness deserted the distant regions of your body, and your body, that beast now gorged with suffering, lay ready to participate in the indifference of marble.

Your very scruples subsided. Our cries ceased to reach you, or, more accurately, changed for you into dream-cries. You were happy now, able to respond by long confident dream-strides that carried you effortlessly towards the enchantment of the plains below. How smoothly you glided into this suddenly merciful world! Guillaumet, you miser! You had made up your mind to deny us your return, to take your pleasures selfishly without us among your white angels in the snows. And then remorse floated up from the depths of your consciousness. The dream was spoilt by the irruption of bothersome details. "I thought of my wife. She would be penniless if she couldn't collect the insurance. Yes, but the company . . ."

When a man vanishes, his legal death is postponed for four years. This awful detail was enough to blot out the other visions. You were lying face downward on a bed of snow that covered a steep mountain slope. With the coming of summer your body would be washed with this slush down into one of the thousand crevasses of the Andes. You knew that. But you also knew that some fifty yards away a rock was jutting up out of the snow. "I thought, if I get up I may be able to reach it. And if I can prop myself up against the rock, they'll find me there next summer."

Once you were on your feet again, you tramped two nights and three days. But you did not then imagine that you would go on much longer:

"I could tell by different signs that the end was coming. For instance, I had to stop every two or three hours to cut my shoes open a bit more and massage my swollen feet. Or maybe my heart would be going too fast. But I was beginning to lose my memory. I had been going on a long time when suddenly I realized that every time I stopped I forgot something. The first time it was a glove. And it was cold! I had put it down in front of me and had forgotten to pick it up. The next time it was my watch. Then my knife. Then my compass. Each time I stopped I stripped myself of something vitally important. I was becoming my own enemy! And I can't tell you how it hurt me when I found that out.

"What saves a man is to take a step. Then another step. It is always the same step, but you have to take it."

"I swear that what I went through, no animal would have gone through." This sentence, the noblest ever spoken, this sentence that defines man's place in the universe, that honors him, that re-establishes the true hierarchy, floated back into my thoughts. Finally you fell asleep. Your consciousness was abolished; but forth from this dismantled, burnt, and shattered body it was to be born again like a flower put forth gradually by the species which itself is born of the luminous pulp of the stars. The body, we may say, then, is but an honest tool, the body is but a servant. And it was in these words, Guillaumet, that you expressed your pride in the honest tool:

"With nothing to eat, after three days on my feet . . . well . . . my heart wasn't going any too well. I was crawling along the side of a sheer wall, hanging over space, digging and kicking out pockets in the ice so that I could hold on, when all of a sudden my heart conked. It hesitated. Started up again. Beat crazily. I said to myself, 'If it hesitates a moment too long, I drop.' I stayed still and listened to myself. Never, never in my life have I listened as carefully to a motor as I listened to my heart, me hanging there. I said to it: 'Come on, old boy. Go to work. Try beating a little.' That's good stuff my heart is made of. It hesitated, but it went on. You don't know how proud I was of that heart."

As I said, in that room in Mendoza where I sat with you, you fell finally into an exhausted sleep. And I thought: If we were to talk to him about his courage, Guillaumet would shrug his shoulders. But it would be just as false to extol his modesty. His place is far beyond that mediocre virtue.

If he shrugs his shoulders, it is because he is no fool. He knows that once men are caught up in an event they cease to be afraid. Only the unknown frightens men. But once a man has faced the unknown, that terror becomes the known.

Especially if it is scrutinized with Guillaumet's lucid gravity. Guillaumet's courage is in the main the product of his honesty. But even this is not his fundamental quality. His moral greatness consists in his sense of responsibility. He knew that he was responsible for himself, for the mails, for the fulfilment of the hopes of his comrades. He was holding in his hands their sorrow and their joy. He was responsible for that new element which the living were constructing and in which he was a participant. Responsible, in as much as his work contributed to it, for the fate of those men.

Guillaumet was one among those bold and generous men who had taken upon themselves the task of spreading their foliage over bold and generous horizons. To be a man is, precisely, to be responsible. It is to feel shame at the sight of what seems to be unmerited misery. It is to take pride in a victory won by one's comrades. It is to feel, when setting one's stone, that one is contributing to the building of the world.

There is a tendency to class such men with toreadors and gamblers. People extol their contempt for death. But I would not give a fig for anybody's contempt for death. If its roots are not sunk deep in an acceptance of responsibility, this contempt for death is the sign either of an impoverished soul or of youthful extravagance.

I once knew a young suicide. I cannot remember what disappointment in love it was which induced him to send a bullet carefully into his heart. I have no notion what literary temptation he had succumbed to when he drew on a pair of white gloves before the shot. But I remember having felt, on learning of this sorry show, an impression not of nobility but of lack of dignity. So! Behind that attractive face, beneath that skull which should have been a treasure chest, there had been nothing, nothing at all. Unless it was the vision of some silly little girl indistinguishable from the rest.

And when I heard of this meagre destiny, I remembered the death of a man. He was a gardener, and he was speaking on his deathbed: "You know, I used to sweat sometimes when I was digging. My rheumatism would pull at my leg, and I would damn myself for a slave. And now, do you know, I'd like to spade and spade. It's beautiful work. A man is free when he is using a spade. And besides, who is going to prune my trees when I am gone?"

That man was leaving behind him a fallow field, a fallow planet. He was bound by ties of love to all cultivable land and to all the trees of the earth. There was a generous man, a prodigal man, a nobleman! There was a man who, battling against death in the name of his Creation, could like Guillaumet be called a man of courage!

· 3 ·

The Tool

Aɴᴅ now, having spoken of the men born of the pilot's craft, I shall say something about the tool with which they work—the airplane. Have you looked at a modern airplane? Have you followed from year to year the evolution of its lines? Have you ever thought, not only about the airplane but about whatever man builds, that all of man's industrial efforts, all his computations and calculations, all the nights spent over working draughts and blueprints, invariably culminate in the production of a thing whose sole and guiding principle is the ultimate principle of simplicity?

It is as if there were a natural law which ordained that to achieve this end, to refine the curve of a piece of furniture, or a ship's keel, or the fuselage of an airplane, until gradually it partakes of the elementary purity of the curve of a human breast or shoulder, there must be the experimentation of several generations of craftsmen. In anything at all, perfection is finally attained not when there is no longer anything to add, but when there is no longer anything to take away, when a body has been stripped down to its nakedness.

It results from this that perfection of invention touches hands with absence of invention, as if that line which the human eye will follow with effortless delight were a line that had not been invented but simply discovered, had in the beginning been hidden by nature and in the end been found by the engineer. There is an ancient myth about the image asleep in the block of marble until it is carefully disengaged by the sculptor. The sculptor must himself feel that he is not so much inventing or shaping the curve of breast or shoulder as delivering the image from its prison.

In this spirit do engineers, physicists concerned with thermodynamics, and the swarm of preoccupied draughtsmen tackle their work. In appearance, but only in appearance, they seem to be polishing surfaces and refining away angles, easing this joint or stabilizing that wing, rendering these parts invisible, so that in the end there is no longer a wing hooked to a framework but a form flawless in its perfection, completely disengaged from its matrix, a sort of spontaneous whole, its parts mysteriously fused together and resembling in their unity a poem.

Meanwhile, startling as it is that all visible evidence of invention should have been refined out of this instrument and that there should be delivered to us an object as natural as a pebble polished by the waves, it is equally wonderful that he who uses this instrument should be able to forget that it is a machine.

There was a time when a flyer sat at the centre of a complicated works. Flight set us factory problems. The indicators that oscillated on the instrument panel warned us of a thousand dangers. But in the machine of today we forget that motors are whirring: the motor, finally, has come to fulfil its function, which is to whirr as a heart beats—and we give no thought to the beating of our heart. Thus, precisely because it is perfect the machine dissembles its own existence instead of forcing itself upon our notice.

And thus, also, the realities of nature resume their pride of place. It is not with metal that the pilot is in contact. Contrary to the vulgar illusion, it is thanks to the metal, and by virtue of it, that the pilot rediscovers nature. As I have already said, the machine does not isolate man from the great problems of nature but plunges him more deeply into them.

Numerous, nevertheless, are the moralists who have

attacked the machine as the source of all the ills we bear, who, creating a fictitious dichotomy, have denounced the mechanical civilization as the enemy of the spiritual civilization.

If what they think were really so, then indeed we should have to despair of man, for it would be futile to struggle against this new advancing chaos. The machine is certainly as irresistible in its advance as those virgin forests that encroach upon equatorial domains. A congeries of motives prevents us from blowing up our spinning mills and reviving the distaff. Gandhi had a try at this sort of revolution: he was as simple-minded as a child trying to empty the sea on to the sand with the aid of a tea-cup.

It is hard for me to understand the language of these pseudo-dreamers. What is it makes them think that the ploughshare torn from the bowels of the earth by perforating machines, forged, tempered, and sharpened in the roar of modern industry, is nearer to man than any other tool of steel? By what sign do they recognize the inhumanity of the machine?

Have they ever really asked themselves this question? The central struggle of men has ever been to understand one another, to join together for the common weal. And it is this very thing that the machine helps them to do! It begins by annihilating time and space.

To me, in France, a friend speaks from America. The energy that brings me his voice is born of dammed-up waters a thousand miles from where he sits. The energy I burn up in listening to him is dispensed in the same instant by a lake formed in the River Yser which, four thousand miles from him and five hundred from me, melts like snow in the action of the turbines. Transport of the mails, transport of the human voice, transport of flickering pictures—in this century as in others our highest accomplishments still have the single aim of bringing men together. Do our dreamers hold that the invention of writing, of printing, of the sailing ship, degraded the human spirit?

It seems to me that those who complain of man's progress confuse ends with means. True, that man who struggles in the unique hope of material gain will harvest nothing worth while. But how can anyone conceive that the machine is an end? It is a tool. As much a tool as is the plough. The microscope is a tool. What disservice do we do the life of the spirit when we analyze the universe through a tool created by the science of optics, or seek to bring together those who love one another and are parted in space?

"Agreed!" my dreamers will say, "but explain to us why it is that a decline in human values has accompanied the rise of the machine?" Oh, I miss the village with its crafts and its folksongs as much as they do! The town fed by Hollywood seems to me, too, impoverished despite its electric street lamps. I quite agree that men lose their creative instincts when they are fed thus without raising a hand. And I can see that it is tempting to accuse industry of this evil.

But we lack perspective for the judgment of transformations that go so deep. What are the hundred years of the history of the machine compared with the two hundred thousand years of the history of man? It was only yesterday that we began to pitch our camp in this country of laboratories and power stations, that we took possession of this new, this still unfinished, house we live in. Everything round us is new and different—our concerns, our working habits, our relations with one another.

Our very psychology has been shaken to its foundations, to its most secret recesses. Our notions of separation, absence, distance, return, are reflections of a new set of realities, though the words themselves remain unchanged. To grasp the meaning of the world of today we use a language created to express the world of yesterday. The life of the past seems to us nearer our true natures, but only for the reason that it is nearer our language.

Every step on the road of progress takes us farther from habits which, as the life of man goes, we had only recently begun to acquire. We are in truth emigrants who have not yet founded our homeland. We Europeans have become again young peoples, without tradition or language of our own. We shall have to age somewhat before we are able to write the folksongs of a new epoch.

Young barbarians still marveling at our new toys—that is what we are. Why else should we race our planes, give prizes to those who fly highest, or fastest? We take no heed to ask ourselves why we race: the race itself is more important than the object.

And this holds true of other things than flying. For the colonial soldier who founds an empire, the meaning of life is conquest. He despises the colonist. But was not the very aim of his conquest the settling of this same colonist?

In the enthusiasm of our rapid mechanical conquests we have overlooked some things. We have perhaps driven men into the service of the machine, instead of building machinery for the service of man. But could anything be more natural? So long as we were engaged in conquest, our spirit was the spirit of conquerors. The time has now come when we must be colonists, must make this house habitable which is still without character.

Little by little the machine will become part of humanity. Read the history of the railways in France, and doubtless elsewhere too: they had all the trouble in the world to tame the people of our villages. The locomotive was an iron monster. Time had to pass before men forgot what it was made of. Mysteriously, life began to run through it, and now it is wrinkled and old. What is it today for the villager except a humble friend who calls every evening at six?

The sailing vessel itself was once a machine born of the calculations of engineers, yet it does not disturb our philosophers. The sloop took its place in the speech of men. There is a poetry of sailing as old as the world. There have always been seamen in recorded time. The man who assumes that there is an essential difference between the sloop and the airplane lacks historic perspective.

Every machine will gradually take on this patina and lose its identity in its function.

Air and water, and not machinery, are the concern of the hydroplane pilot about to take off. The motors are running free and the plane is already ploughing the surface of the sea. Under the dizzying whirl of the scythe-like propellers, clusters of silvery water bloom and drown the flotation gear. The element smacks the sides of the hull with a sound like a gong, and the pilot can sense this tumult in the quivering of his body. He feels the ship charging itself with power as from second to second it picks up speed. He feels the development, in these fifteen tons of matter, of a maturity that is about to make flight possible. He closes his hands over the controls, and little by little in his bare palms he receives the gift of this power. The metal organs of the controls, progressively as this gift is made him, become the messengers of the power in his hands. And when his power is ripe, then, in a gesture gentler than the culling of a flower, the pilot severs the ship from the water and establishes it in the air.

· 4 ·

The Elements

WHEN Joseph Conrad described a typhoon he said very little about towering waves, or darkness, or the whistling of the wind in the shrouds. He knew better. Instead, he took his reader down into the hold of the vessel, packed with emigrant coolies, where the rolling and the pitching of the ship had ripped up and scattered their bags and bundles, burst open their boxes, and flung their humble belongings into a crazy heap. Family treasures painfully collected in a lifetime of poverty, pitiful mementoes so alike that nobody but their owners could have told them apart, had lost their identity and lapsed into chaos, into anonymity, into an amorphous magma. It was this human drama that Conrad described when he painted a typhoon.

Every airline pilot has flown through tornadoes, has returned out of them to the fold—to the little restaurant in Toulouse where we sat in peace under the watchful eye of the waitress—and there, recognizing his powerlessness to convey what he has been through, has given up the idea of describing hell. His descriptions, his gestures, his big words would have made the rest of us smile as if we were listening to a little boy bragging. And necessarily so. The cyclone of which I am about to speak was, physically, much the most brutal and overwhelming experience I ever underwent; and yet beyond a certain point I do not know how to convey its violence except by piling one adjective on another, so that in the end I should convey no impression at all—unless perhaps that of an embarrassing taste for exaggeration.

It took me some time to grasp the fundamental reason for this powerlessness, which is simply that I should be trying to describe a catastrophe that never took place. The reason why writers fail when they attempt to evoke horror is that horror is something invented after the fact, when one is re-creating the experience over again in the memory. Horror does not manifest itself in the world of reality. And so, in beginning my story of a revolt of the elements which I myself lived through I

have no feeling that I shall write something which you
will find dramatic.

I had taken off from the field at Trelew and was
flying down to Comodoro-Rivadavia, in the Patagonian
Argentine. Here the crust of the earth is as dented
as an old boiler. The high-pressure regions over
the Pacific send the winds past a gap in the Andes
into a corridor fifty miles wide through which they rush
to the Atlantic in a strangled and accelerated buffeting
that scrapes the surface of everything in their path. The
sole vegetation visible in this barren landscape is a plantation of oil derricks looking like the after-effects of a
forest fire. Towering over the round hills on which the
winds have left a residue of stony gravel, there rises a
chain of prow-shaped, saw-toothed, razor-edged mountains stripped by the elements down to the bare rock.

For three months of the year the speed of these winds
at ground level is up to a hundred miles an hour. We
who flew the route knew that once we had crossed the
marshes of Trelew and had reached the threshold of the
zone they swept, we should recognize the winds from
afar by a grey-blue tint in the atmosphere at the sight of
which we would tighten our belts and shoulder-straps in
preparation for what was coming. From then on we had
an hour of stiff fighting and of stumbling again and again
into invisible ditches of air. This was manual labor, and
our muscles felt it pretty much as if we had been car-

rying a longshoreman's load. But it lasted only an hour. Our machines stood up under it. We had no fear of wings suddenly dropping off. Visibility was generally good, and not a problem. This section of the line was a stint, yes; it was certainly not a drama.

But on this particular day I did not like the color of the sky.

The sky was blue. Pure blue. Too pure. A hard blue sky that shone over the scraped and barren world while the fleshless vertebrae of the mountain chain flashed in the sunlight. Not a cloud. The blue sky glittered like a new-honed knife. I felt in advance the vague distaste that accompanies the prospect of physical exertion. The purity of the sky upset me. Give me a good black storm in which the enemy is plainly visible. I can measure its extent and prepare myself for its attack. I can get my hands on my adversary. But when you are flying very high in clear weather the shock of a blue storm is as disturbing as if something collapsed that had been holding up your ship in the air. It is the only time when a pilot feels that there is a gulf beneath his ship.

Another thing bothered me. I could see on a level with the mountain peaks not a haze, not a mist, not a sandy fog, but a sort of ash-colored streamer in the sky. I did not like the look of that scarf of filings scraped off the surface of the earth and borne out to sea by the wind. I tightened my leather harness as far as it would go and I steered the ship with one hand while with the other I hung on to the longéron that ran alongside my seat. I was still flying in remarkably calm air.

Very soon came a slight tremor. As every pilot knows, there are secret little quiverings that foretell your real storm. No rolling, no pitching. No swing to speak of. The flight continues horizontal and rectilinear. But you have felt a warning drum on the wings of your plane, little intermittent rappings scarcely audible and infinitely brief, little cracklings from time to time as if there were traces of gunpowder in the air.

And then everything round me blew up.

Concerning the next couple of minutes I have nothing to say. All that I can find in my memory is a few rudimentary notions, fragments of thoughts, direct observations. I cannot compose them into a dramatic recital because there was no drama. The best I can do is to line them up in a kind of chronological order.

In the first place, I was standing still. Having banked right in order to correct a sudden drift, I saw the landscape freeze abruptly where it was and remain jiggling on the same spot. I was making no headway. My wings had ceased to nibble into the outline of the earth. I could see the earth buckle, pivot—but it stayed put. The plane was skidding as if on a toothless cogwheel.

Meanwhile I had the absurd feeling that I had exposed myself completely to the enemy. All those peaks, those crests, those teeth that were cutting into the wind and unleashing its gusts in my direction, seemed to me so many guns pointed straight at my defenseless person. I was slow to think, but the thought did come to me that I ought to give up altitude and make for one of the neighboring valleys where I might take shelter against a mountainside. As a matter of fact, whether I liked it or not I was being helplessly sucked down towards the earth.

Trapped this way in the first breaking waves of a cyclone about which I learned, twenty minutes later, that at sea level it was blowing at the fantastic rate of one hundred and fifty miles an hour, I certainly had no impression of tragedy. Now, as I write, if I shut my eyes, if I forget the plane and the flight and try to express the plain truth about what was happening to me, I find that I felt weighed down, I felt like a porter carrying a slippery load, grabbing one object in a jerky movement that sent another slithering down, so that, overcome by exasperation, the porter is tempted to let the whole load drop. There is a kind of law of the shortest distance to the image, a psychological law by which the event to which one is subjected is visualized in a symbol that represents its swiftest summing up: I was a man who, carrying a pile of plates, had slipped on a waxed floor and let his scaffolding of porcelain crash.

I found myself imprisoned in a valley. My discomfort was not less, it was greater. I grant you that a down current has never killed anybody, that the expression "flattened out by a down current" belongs to journalism and not to the language of flyers. How could air possibly pierce the ground? But here I was in a valley at the wheel of a ship that was three-quarters out of my control. Ahead of me a rocky prow swung to left and right, rose suddenly high in the air for a second like a wave over my head, and then plunged down below my horizon.

Horizon? There was no longer a horizon. I was in the wings of a theatre cluttered up with bits of scenery. Vertical, oblique, horizontal, all of plane geometry was awhirl. A hundred transversal valleys were muddled in a jumble of perspectives. Whenever I seemed about to take my bearings a new eruption would swing me round in a circle or send me tumbling wing over wing and I would have to try all over again to get clear of all this rubbish. Two ideas came into my mind. One was a discovery: for the first time I understood the cause of certain accidents in the mountains when no fog was present to explain them. For a single second, in a waltzing landscape like this, the flyer had been unable to distinguish between vertical mountainsides and horizontal planes. The other idea was a fixation: The sea is flat: I shall not hook anything out at sea.

I banked—or should I use that word to indicate a vague and stubborn jockeying through the east-west valleys? Still nothing pathetic to report. I was wrestling with chaos, was wearing myself out in a battle with chaos, struggling to keep in the air a gigantic house of cards that kept collapsing despite all I could do. Scarcely the faintest twinge of fear went through me when one of the walls of my prison rose suddenly like a tidal wave over my head. My heart hardly skipped a beat when I was tripped up by one of the whirling eddies of air that the sharp ridge darted into my ship. If I felt anything unmistakably in the haze of confused feelings and notions that came over me each time one of these powder magazines blew up, it was a feeling of respect. I respected that sharp-toothed ridge. I respected that peak. I respected that dome. I respected that transversal valley opening out into my valley and about to toss me God knew how violently as soon as its torrent of wind flowed into the one on which I was being borne along.

What I was struggling against, I discovered, was not the wind but the ridge itself, the crest, the rocky peak. Despite my distance from it, it was the wall of rock I was fighting with. By some trick of invisible prolongation, by the play of a secret set of muscles, this was what was pummeling me. It was against this that I was butting my head. Before me on the right I recognized the peak of Salamanca, a perfect cone which, I knew, dominated the sea. It cheered me to think I was about to escape out to sea. But first I should have to wrestle with the gale off that peak, try to avoid its down-crushing blow. The peak of Salamanca was a giant. I was filled with respect for the peak of Salamanca.

There had been granted me one second of respite. Two seconds. Something was collecting itself into a knot, coiling itself up, growing taut. I sat amazed. I opened astonished eyes. My whole plane seemed to be shivering, spreading outward, swelling up. Horizontal and stationary it was, yet lifted before I knew it fifteen hundred feet straight into the air in a kind of apotheosis. I who for forty minutes had not been able to climb higher than two hundred feet off the ground was suddenly able to look down on the enemy. The plane quivered as if in boiling water. I could see the wide waters of the ocean. The valley opened out into this ocean, his salvation.—And at that very moment, without any warning whatever, half a mile from Salamanca, I was suddenly struck straight in the midriff by the gale off that peak and sent hurtling out to sea.

There I was, throttle wide open, facing the coast. At right angles to the coast and facing it. A lot had happened in a single minute. In the first place, I had not flown out to sea. I had been spat out to sea by a monstrous cough, vomited out of my valley as from the mouth of a howitzer. When, what seemed to me instantly, I banked in order to put myself where I wanted to be in respect of the coast-line, I saw that the coast-line was a mere blur, a characterless strip of blue; and I was five miles out to sea. The mountain range stood up like a crenelated fortress against the pure sky while the cyclone crushed me down to the surface of the waters. How hard that wind was blowing I found out as soon as I tried to climb, as soon as I became conscious of my disastrous mistake: throttle wide open, engines running at my maximum, which was one hundred and fifty miles an hour, my plane hanging sixty feet over the water, I was unable to budge. When a wind like this one attacks a tropical forest it swirls through the branches like a flame, twists them into corkscrews, and uproots giant trees as if they were radishes. Here, bounding off the mountain range, it was leveling out the sea.

Hanging on with all the power in my engines, face to the coast, face to that wind where each gap in the teeth of the range sent forth a stream of air like a long reptile, I felt as if I were clinging to the tip of a monstrous whip that was cracking over the sea.

In this latitude the South American continent is narrow and the Andes are not far from the Atlantic. I was struggling not merely against the whirling winds that blew off the east-coast range, but more likely also against a whole sky blown down upon me off the peaks of the Andean chain. For the first time in four years of airline flying I began to worry about the strength of my wings. Also, I was fearful of bumping the sea—not because of the down currents which, at sea level, would necessarily provide me with a horizontal air mattress, but because of the helplessly acrobatic positions in which this wind was buffeting me. Each time that I was tossed I became afraid that I might be unable to straighten out. Besides, there was a chance that I should find myself out of fuel and simply drown. I kept expecting the gasoline pumps to stop priming, and indeed the plane was so violently shaken up that in the half-filled tanks as well as in the gas lines the gasoline was sloshing round, not coming through, and the engines, instead of their steady roar, were sputtering in a sort of dot-and-dash series of uncertain growls.

I hung on, meanwhile, to the controls of my heavy transport plane, my attention monopolized by the physical struggle and my mind occupied by the very simplest thoughts. I was feeling practically nothing as I stared down at the imprint made by the wind on the sea. I saw a series of great white puddles, each perhaps eight hundred yards in extent. They were running towards me at a speed of one hundred and fifty miles an hour where the down-surging windspouts broke against the surface of the sea in a succession of horizontal explosions. The sea was white and it was green—white with the whiteness of crushed sugar and green in puddles the color of emeralds. In this tumult one wave was indistinguishable from another. Torrents of air were pouring down upon the sea. The winds were sweeping past in giant gusts as when, before the autumn harvests, they blow a great flowing change of color over a wheatfield. Now and

again the water went incongruously transparent between the white pools, and I could see a green and black
sea-bottom. And then the great glass of the sea would
be shattered anew into a thousand glittering fragments.

It seemed hopeless. In twenty minutes of struggle I
had not moved forward a hundred yards. What was
more, with flying as hard as it was out here five miles
from the coast, I wondered how I could possibly buck
the winds along the shore, assuming I was able to fight
my way in. I was a perfect target for the enemy there
on shore. Fear, however, was out of the question. I was
incapable of thinking. I was emptied of everything except the vision of a very simple act. I must straighten
out. Straighten out. Straighten out.

There were moments of respite, nevertheless. I dare
say those moments themselves were equal to the worst
storms I had hitherto met, but by comparison with the
cyclone they were moments of relaxation. The urgency
of fighting off the wind was not quite so great. And I
could tell when these intervals were coming. It was not
I who moved towards those zones of relative calm, those
almost green oases clearly painted on the sea, but they
that flowed towards me. I could read clearly in the waters the advertisement of a habitable province. And with
each interval of repose the power to feel and to think
was restored to me. Then, in those moments, I began to
feel I was doomed. Then was the time that little by

little I began to tremble for myself. So much so that each time I saw the unfurling of a new wave of the white offensive I was seized by a brief spasm of panic which lasted until the exact instant when, on the edge of that bubbling cauldron, I bumped into the invisible wall of wind. That restored me to numbness again.

Up! I wanted to be higher up. The next time I saw one of those green zones of calm it seemed to me deeper than before and I began to be hopeful of getting out. If I could climb high enough, I thought, I would find other currents in which I could make some headway. I took advantage of the truce to essay a swift climb. It was hard. The enemy had not weakened. Three hundred feet. Six hundred feet. If I could get up to three thousand feet I was safe, I said to myself. But there on the horizon I saw again that white pack unleashed in my direction. I gave it up. I did not want them at my throat again; I did not want to be caught off balance. But it was too late. The first blow sent me rolling over and over and the sky became a slippery dome on which I could not find a footing.

One has a pair of hands and they obey. How are one's orders transmitted to one's hands?

I had made a discovery that horrified me: my hands were numb. My hands were dead. They sent me no message. Probably they had been numb a long time and

I had not noticed it. The pity was that I had noticed it, had raised the question. That was serious.

Lashed by the wind, the wings of the plane had been dragging and jerking at the cables by which they were controlled from the wheel, and the wheel in my hands had not ceased jerking a single second. I had been gripping the wheel with all my might for forty minutes, fearful lest the strain snap the cables. So desperate had been my grip that now I could not feel my hands.

What a discovery! My hands were not my own. I looked at them and decided to lift a finger: it obeyed me. I looked away and issued the same order: now I could not feel whether the finger had obeyed or not. No message had reached me. I thought: "Suppose my hands were to open: how would I know it?" I swung my head round and looked again: my hands were still locked round the wheel. Nevertheless, I was afraid. How can a man tell the difference between the sight of a hand opening and the decision to open that hand, when there is no longer an exchange of sensations between the hand and the brain? How can one tell the difference between an image and an act of the will? Better stop thinking of the picture of open hands. Hands live a life of their own. Better not offer them this monstrous temptation. And I began to chant a silly litany which went on uninterruptedly until this flight was over. A single thought. A single image. A single phrase tirelessly chanted over and over again: "I shut my hands. I shut my hands. I shut my hands." All of me was condensed into that phrase and for me the white sea, the whirling eddies, the saw-toothed range ceased to exist. There was only "I shut my hands." There was no danger, no cyclone, no land unattained. Somewhere there was a pair of rubber hands which, once they let go the wheel, could not possibly come alive in time to recover from the tumbling drop into the sea.

I had no thoughts. I had no feelings except the feeling of being emptied out. My strength was draining out of me and so was my impulse to go on fighting. The engines continued their dot-and-dash sputterings, their little crashing noises that were like the intermittent cracklings of a ripping canvas. Whenever they were silent longer than a second I felt as if a heart had stopped beating. There! that's the end. No, they've started up again.

The thermometer on the wing, I happened to see, stood at twenty below zero, but I was bathed in sweat from head to foot. My face was running with perspiration. What a dance! Later I was to discover that my storage batteries had been jerked out of their steel flanges and hurtled up through the roof of the plane. I did not know then, either, that the ribs on my wings had come unglued and that certain of my steel cables had been sawed down to the last thread. And I continued to feel strength and will oozing out of me. Any minute now I should be overcome by the indifference born of utter weariness and by the mortal yearning to take my rest.

What can I say about this? Nothing. My shoulders ached. Very painfully. As if I had been carrying too many sacks too heavy for me. I leaned forward. Through a green transparency I saw sea-bottom so close that I could make out all the details. Then the wind's hand brushed the picture away.

In an hour and twenty minutes I had succeeded in climbing to nine hundred feet. A little to the south—that is, on my left—I could see a long trail on the surface of the sea, a sort of blue stream. I decided to let myself drift as far down as that stream. Here where I was, facing west, I was as good as motionless, unable either to advance or retreat. If I could reach that blue pathway, which must be lying in the shelter of something not the cyclone, I might be able to move in slowly to the coast. So I let myself drift to the left. I had the feeling, meanwhile, that the wind's violence had perhaps slackened.

It took me an hour to cover the five miles to shore There in the shelter of a long cliff I was able to finish my journey south. Thereafter I succeeded in keeping enough altitude to fly inland to the field that was my destination. I was able to stay up at nine hundred feet. It was very stormy, but nothing like the cyclone I had come out of. That was over.

On the ground I saw a platoon of soldiers. They had

been sent down to watch for me. I landed near by and we were a whole hour getting the plane into the hangar. I climbed out of the cockpit and walked off. There was nothing to say. I was very sleepy. I kept moving my fingers, but they stayed numb. I could not collect my thoughts enough to decide whether or not I had been afraid. Had I been afraid? I couldn't say. I had witnessed a strange sight. What strange sight? I couldn't say. The sky was blue and the sea was white. I felt I ought to tell someone about it since I was back from so far away! But I had no grip on what I had been through. "Imagine a white sea . . . very white . . . whiter still." You cannot convey things to people by piling up adjectives, by stammering.

You cannot convey anything because there is nothing to convey. My shoulders were aching. My insides felt as if they had been crushed in by a terrible weight. You cannot make drama out of that, or out of the cone-shaped peak of Salamanca. That peak was charged like a powder magazine; but if I said so people would laugh. I would myself. I respected the peak of Salamanca. That is my story. And it is not a story.

There is nothing dramatic in the world, nothing pathetic, except in human relations. The day after I landed I might get emotional, might dress up my adventure by imagining that I who was alive and walking on earth was living through the hell of a cyclone. But that would be cheating, for the man who fought tooth and nail against that cyclone had nothing in common with the fortunate man alive the next day. He was far too busy.

I came away with very little booty indeed, with no more than this meagre discovery, this contribution: How can one tell an act of the will from a simple image when there is no transmission of sensation?

I could perhaps succeed in upsetting you if I told you some story of a child unjustly punished. As it is, I have involved you in a cyclone, probably without upsetting you in the least. This is no novel experience for any of us. Every week men sit comfortably at the cinema and look on at the bombardment of some Shanghai or other, some Guernica, and marvel without a trace of horror at the long fringes of ash and soot that twist their slow way into the sky from those man-made volcanoes. Yet we all know that together with the grain in the granaries, with the heritage of generations of men, with the treasures of families, it is the burning flesh of children and their elders that, dissipated in smoke, is slowly fertilizing those black cumuli.

The physical drama itself cannot touch us until some one points out its spiritual sense.

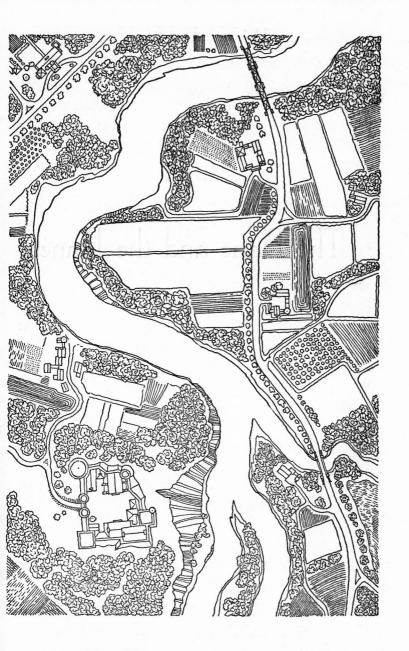

· 5 ·

The Plane and the Planet

THE airplane has unveiled for us the true face of the earth. For centuries, highways had been deceiving us. We were like that queen who determined to move among her subjects so that she might learn for herself whether or not they rejoiced in her reign. Her courtiers took advantage of her innocence to garland the road she traveled and set dancers in her path. Led forward on their halter, she saw nothing of her kingdom and could not know that over the countryside the famished were cursing her.

Even so have we been making our way along the

winding roads. Roads avoid the barren lands, the rocks, the sands. They shape themselves to man's needs and run from stream to stream. They lead the farmer from his barns to his wheatfields, receive at the thresholds of stables the sleepy cattle and pour them forth at dawn into meadows of alfalfa. They join village to village, for between villages marriages are made.

And even when a road hazards its way over the desert, you will see it make a thousand détours to take its pleasure at the oases. Thus, led astray by the divagations of roads, as by other indulgent fictions, having in the course of our travels skirted so many well-watered lands, so many orchards, so many meadows, we have from the beginning of time embellished the picture of our prison. We have elected to believe that our planet was merciful and fruitful.

But a cruel light has blazed, and our sight has been sharpened. The plane has taught us to travel as the crow flies. Scarcely have we taken off when we abandon these winding highways that slope down to watering troughs and stables or run away to towns dreaming in the shade of their trees. Freed henceforth from this happy servitude, delivered from the need of fountains, we set our course for distant destinations. And then, only, from the height of our rectilinear trajectories, do we discover the essential foundation, the fundament of rock and sand and salt in which here and there and from time to time life like a little moss in the crevices of ruins has risked its precarious existence.

We to whom humble journeyings were once permitted have now been transformed into physicists, biologists, students of the civilizations that beautify the depths of valleys and now and again, by some miracle, bloom like gardens where the climate allows. We are able to judge man in cosmic terms, scrutinize him through our portholes as through instruments of the laboratory. I remember a few of these scenes.

I

The pilot flying towards the Straits of Magellan sees below him, a little to the south of the Gallegos River, an ancient lava flow, an erupted waste of a thickness of sixty feet that crushes down the plain on which it has congealed. Farther south he meets a second flow, then a third; and thereafter every hump on the globe, every mound a few hundred feet high, carries a crater in its flank. No Vesuvius rises up to reign in the clouds; merely, flat on the plain, a succession of gaping howitzer mouths.

This day, as I fly, the lava world is calm. There is something surprising in the tranquillity of this deserted landscape where once a thousand volcanoes boomed to each other in their great subterranean organs and spat forth their fire. I fly over a world mute and abandoned, strewn with black glaciers.

South of these glaciers there are yet older volcanoes veiled with the passing of time in a golden sward. Here and there a tree rises out of a crevice like a plant out of a cracked pot. In the soft and yellow light the plain appears as luxuriant as a garden; the short grass seems to civilize it, and round its giant throats there is scarcely a swelling to be seen. A hare scampers off; a bird wheels in the air; life has taken possession of a new planet where the decent loam of our earth has at last spread over the surface of the star.

Finally, crossing the line into Chile, a little north of Punta Arenas, you come to the last of the craters, and here the mouths have been stopped with earth. A silky turf lies snug over the curves of the volcanoes, and all is suavity in the scene. Each fissure in the crust is sutured up by this tender flax. The earth is smooth, the slopes are gentle; one forgets the travail that gave them birth. This turf effaces from the flanks of the hillocks the sombre sign of their origin.

We have reached the most southerly habitation of the world, a town born of the chance presence of a little mud between the timeless lava and the austral ice. So near the black scoria, how thrilling it is to feel the miraculous nature of man! What a strange encounter! Who knows how, or why, man visits these gardens ready to hand, habitable for so short a time—a geologic age—for a single day blessed among days?

I landed in the peace of evening. Punta Arenas! I leaned against a fountain and looked at the girls in the square. Standing there within a couple of feet of their grace, I felt more poignantly than ever the human mystery.

In a world in which life so perfectly responds to life, where flowers mingle with flowers in the wind's eye, where the swan is the familiar of all swans, man alone builds his isolation. What a space between men their spiritual natures create! A girl's reverie isolates her from me, and how shall I enter into it? What can one know of a girl who passes, walking with slow steps homeward, eyes lowered, smiling to herself, filled with adorable inventions and with fables? Out of the thoughts, the voice, the silences of a lover, she can form an empire, and thereafter she sees in all the world but him a people of barbarians. More surely than if she were on another planet, I feel her to be locked up in her language, in her secret, in her habits, in the singing echoes of her memory. Born yesterday of the volcanoes, of greenswards, of brine of the sea, she walks here already half divine.

Punta Arenas! I lean against a fountain. Old women come up to draw water: of their drama I shall know nothing but these gestures of farm servants. A child, his head against a wall, weeps in silence: there will remain of him in my memory only a beautiful child forever inconsolable. I am a stranger. I know nothing. I do not enter into their empires. Man in the presence of man is as solitary as in the face of a wide winter sky in which there sweeps, never to be tamed, a flight of trumpeting geese.

How shallow is the stage on which this vast drama of human hates and joys and friendships is played! Whence do men draw this passion for eternity, flung by chance as they are upon a scarcely cooled bed of lava, threatened from the beginning by the deserts that are to be, and under the constant menace of the snows? Their civilizations are but fragile gildings: a volcano can blot them out, a new sea, a sand-storm.

This town seemed to be built upon a true humus, a soil one might imagine to be as rich as the wheatlands of the Beauce. These men live heedless of the fact that, here as elsewhere, life is a luxury; and that nowhere on the globe is the soil really rich beneath the feet of men.

Yet, ten miles from Punta Arenas there is a lake that ought to be reminding them of this. Surrounded by stunted trees and squat huts, as modest as a pool in a farm-yard, this lake is subject to the preternatural pull of the tides. Night and day, among the peaceful realities of swaying reeds and playing children, it performs its slow respiration, obedient to unearthly laws. Beneath the glassy surface, beneath the motionless ice, beneath the keel of the single dilapidated bark on the waters, the energy of the moon is at work. Ocean eddies stir in the depths of this black mass. Strange digestions take their peristaltic course there and down as far as the Straits of Magellan, under the thin layer of grasses and flowers. This lake that is a hundred yards wide, that laps the threshold of a town which seems to be built on man's own earth and where men believe themselves secure, beats with the pulse of the sea.

II

But by the grace of the airplane I have known a more extraordinary experience than this, and have been made to ponder with even more bewilderment the fact that this earth that is our home is yet in truth a wandering star.

A minor accident had forced me down in the Rio de Oro region, in Spanish Africa. Landing on one of those table-lands of the Sahara which fall away steeply at the sides, I found myself on the flat top of the frustrum of a cone, an isolated vestige of a plateau that had crumbled round the edges. In this part of the Sahara such truncated cones are visible from the air every hundred miles or so, their smooth surfaces always at about the same altitude above the desert and their geologic substance always identical. The surface sand is composed of minute and distinct shells; but progressively as you dig along a vertical section, the shells become more fragmentary, tend to cohere, and at the base of the cone form a pure calcareous deposit.

Without question, I was the first human being ever to wander over this . . . this iceberg: its sides were remarkably steep, no Arab could have climbed them, and no European had as yet ventured into this wild region.

I was thrilled by the virginity of a soil which no step of man or beast had sullied. I lingered there, startled by this silence that never had been broken. The first star began to shine, and I said to myself that this pure surface had lain here thousands of years in sight only of the stars.

But suddenly my musings on this white sheet and these shining stars were endowed with a singular significance. I had kicked against a hard, black stone, the size of a man's fist, a sort of moulded rock of lava incredibly present on the surface of a bed of shells a thousand feet deep. A sheet spread beneath an apple-tree can receive only apples; a sheet spread beneath the stars can receive only star-dust. Never had a stone fallen from the skies made known its origin so unmistakably.

And very naturally, raising my eyes, I said to myself that from the height of this celestial apple-tree there must have dropped other fruits, and that I should find them exactly where they fell, since never from the beginning of time had anything been present to displace them.

Excited by my adventure, I picked up one and then a second and then a third of these stones, finding them at about the rate of one stone to the acre. And here is where my adventure became magical, for in a striking foreshortening of time that embraced thousands of years, I had become the witness of this miserly rain from the stars. The marvel of marvels was that there on the rounded back of the planet, between this magnetic sheet and those stars, a human consciousness was present in which as in a mirror that rain could be reflected.

III

Once, in this same mineral Sahara, I was taught that a dream might partake of the miraculous. Again I had been forced down, and until day dawned I was help-less. Hillocks of sand offered up their luminous slopes to the moon, and blocks of shadow rose to share the sands with the light. Over the deserted work-yard of darkness and moonray there reigned a peace as of work sus-pended and a silence like a trap, in which I fell asleep.

When I opened my eyes I saw nothing but the pool of nocturnal sky, for I was lying on my back with out-stretched arms, face to face with that hatchery of stars. Only half awake, still unaware that those depths were sky, having no roof between those depths and me, no branches to screen them, no root to cling to, I was seized with vertigo and felt myself as if flung forth and plunging downward like a diver.

But I did not fall. From nape to heel I discovered my-self bound to earth. I felt a sort of appeasement in sur-rendering to it my weight. Gravitation had become as sovereign as love. The earth, I felt, was supporting my back, sustaining me, lifting me up, transporting me through the immense void of night. I was glued to our planet by a pressure like that with which one is glued to the side of a car on a curve. I leaned with joy against this admirable breast-work, this solidity, this security, feel-ing against my body this curving bridge of my ship.

So convinced was I that I was in motion, that I should have heard without astonishment, rising from below, a creaking of something material adjusting itself to the effort, that groaning of old sailing vessels as they heel, that long sharp cry drawn from pinnaces complaining of their handling. But silence continued in the layers of the earth, and this density that I could feel at my shoulders continued harmonious, sustained, unaltered through eternity. I was as much the inhabitant of this homeland as the bodies of dead galley-slaves, weighted with lead, were the inhabitants of the sea.

I lay there pondering my situation, lost in the desert and in danger, naked between sky and sand, withdrawn by too much silence from the poles of my life. I knew that I should wear out days and weeks returning to them if I were not sighted by some plane, or if next day the

Moors did not find and murder me. Here I possessed nothing in the world. I was no more than a mortal strayed between sand and stars, conscious of the single blessing of breathing. And yet I discovered myself filled with dreams.

They came to me soundlessly, like the waters of a spring, and in the beginning I could not understand the sweetness that was invading me. There was neither voice nor vision, but the presentiment of a presence, of a warmth very close and already half guessed. Then I began to grasp what was going on, and shutting my eyes I gave myself up to the enchantments of my memory.

Somewhere there was a park dark with firs and lin-den-trees and an old house that I loved. It mattered little that it was far away, that it could not warm me in my flesh, nor shelter me, reduced here to the rôle of dream. It was enough that it existed to fill my night with its presence. I was no longer this body flung up on a strand; I oriented myself; I was the child of this house, filled with the memory of its odors, with the cool breath of its vestibules, with the voices that had animated it, even to the very frogs in the pools that came here to be with me. I needed these thousand landmarks to identify my-self, to discover of what absences the savor of this desert was composed, to find a meaning in this silence made of a thousand silences, where the very frogs were silent.

No, I was no longer lodged between sand and stars. I was no longer receiving from this scene its chill mes-

sage. And I had found out at last the origin of the feeling of eternity that came over me in this wilderness. I
had been wrong to believe it was part of sky and sand.
I saw again the great stately cupboards of our house.
Their doors opened to display piles of linen as white as
snow. They opened on frozen stores of snow. The old
housekeeper trotted like a rat from one cupboard to the
next, forever counting, folding, unfolding, re-counting
the white linen; exclaiming, "Oh, good Heavens, how
terrible!" at each sign of wear which threatened the
eternity of the house; running instantly to burn out her
eyes under a lamp so that the woof of these altar cloths
should be repaired, these three-master's sails be mended,
in the service of something greater than herself—a god,
a ship.

Ah, I owe you a page, Mademoiselle! When I came
home from my first journeyings I found you needle in
hand, up to the knees in your white surplices, each year
a little more wrinkled, a little more round-shouldered,
still preparing for our slumbers those sheets without
creases, for our dinners those cloths without seams, those
feasts of crystal and of snow.

I would go up to see you in your sewing-room, would
sit down beside you and tell you of the dangers I had
run in order that I might thrill you, open your eyes to
the world, corrupt you. You would say that I hadn't
changed a whit. Already as a child I had torn my shirts

—"How terrible!"—and skinned my knees, coming home as day fell to be bandaged.

No, Mademoiselle, no! I have not come back from the other end of the park but from the other end of the world! I have brought back with me the acrid smell of solitude, the tumult of sand-storms, the blazing moonlight of the tropics! "Of course!" you would say. "Boys *will* run about, break their bones and think themselves great fellows."

No, Mademoiselle, no! I have seen a good deal more than the shadows in our park. If you knew how insignificant these shadows are, how little they mean beside the sands, the granite, the virgin forests, the vast swamplands of the earth! Do you realize that there are lands on the globe where, when men meet you, they bring up their rifles to their cheeks? Do you know that there are deserts on earth where men lie down on freezing nights to sleep without roof or bed or snowy sheet? "What a wild lad!" you would say.

I could no more shake her faith than I could have shaken the faith of a candle-woman in a church. I pitied her humble destiny which had made her blind and deaf.

But that night in the Sahara, naked between the stars and the sand, I did her justice.

What is going on inside me I cannot tell. In the sky a thousand stars are magnetized, and I lie glued by the swing of the planet to the sand. A different weight brings me back to myself. I feel the weight of my body drawing me towards so many things. My dreams are more real than these dunes, than that moon, than these presences. My civilization is an empire more imperious than this empire. The marvel of a house is not that it shelters or warms a man, nor that its walls belong to him. It is that it leaves its trace on the language. Let it remain a sign. Let it form, deep in the heart, that obscure range from which, as waters from a spring, are born our dreams.

Sahara, my Sahara! You have been bewitched by an old woman at a spinning-wheel!

· 6 ·

Oasis

I HAVE already said so much about the desert that before speaking of it again I should like to describe an
oasis. The oasis that comes into my mind is not,
however, remote in the deep Sahara. One of the miracles
of the airplane is that it plunges a man directly into the
heart of mystery. You are a biologist studying, through
your porthole, the human ant-hill, scrutinizing objec-
tively those towns seated in their plain at the centre of
their highways which go off like the spokes of a wheel
and, like arteries, nourish them with the quintessence of
the fields. A needle trembles on your manometer, and

this green clump below you becomes a universe. You are the prisoner of a greensward in a slumbering park.

Space is not the measure of distance. A garden wall at home may enclose more secrets than the Great Wall of China, and the soul of a little girl is better guarded by silence than the Sahara's oases by the surrounding sands. I dropped down to earth once somewhere in the world. It was near Concordia, in the Argentine, but it might have been anywhere at all, for mystery is everywhere.

A minor mishap had forced me down in a field, and I was far from dreaming that I was about to live through a fairy-tale. The old Ford in which I was driven to town betokened nothing extraordinary, and the same was to be said for the unremarkable couple who took me in.

"We shall be glad to put you up for the night," they said.

But round a corner of the road, in the moonlight, I saw a clump of trees, and behind those trees a house. What a queer house! Squat, massive, almost a citadel guarding behind its tons of stone I knew not what treasure. From the very threshold this legendary castle promised an asylum as assured, as peaceful, as secret as a monastery.

Then two young girls appeared. They seemed astonished to see me, examined me gravely as if they had been two judges posted on the confines of a forbidden kingdom, and while the younger of them sulked and tapped the ground with a green switch, they were introduced:

"Our daughters."

The girls shook hands without a word but with a curious air of defiance, and disappeared. I was amused and I was charmed. It was all as simple and silent and furtive as the first word of a secret.

"The girls are shy," their father said, and we went into the house.

One thing that I had loved in Paraguay was the ironic grass that showed the tip of its nose between the pavements of the capital, that slipped in on behalf of the invisible but ever-present virgin forest to see if man still held the town, if the hour had not come to send all these stones tumbling.

I liked the particular kind of dilapidation which in Paraguay was the expression of an excess of wealth. But here, in Concordia, I was filled with wonder. Here everything was in a state of decay, but adorably so, like an old oak covered with moss and split in places with age, like a wooden bench on which generations of lovers had come to sit and which had grown sacred. The wainscoting was worn, the hinges rusted, the chairs rickety. And yet, though nothing had ever been repaired, everything had been scoured with zeal. Everything was clean, waxed, gleaming.

The drawing-room had about it something extraordinarily intense, like the face of a wrinkled old lady. The walls were cracked, the ceiling stripped; and most bewildering of all in this bewildering house was the floor:

it had simply caved in. Waxed, varnished and polished though it was, it swayed like a ship's gangway. A strange house, evoking no neglect, no slackness, but rather an extraordinary respect. Each passing year had added something to its charm, to the complexity of its visage and its friendly atmosphere, as well as to the dangers encountered on the journey from the drawing-room to the dining-room.

"Careful!"

There was a hole in the floor; and I was warned that if I stepped into it I might easily break a leg. This was said as simply as "Don't stroke the dog, he bites." Nobody was responsible for the hole, it was the work of time. There was something lordly about this sovereign contempt for apologies.

Nobody said, "We could have these holes repaired; we are well enough off; but . . ." And neither did they say—which was true enough—"we have taken this house from the town under a thirty-year lease. They should look after the repairs. But they won't, and we won't, so . . ." They disdained explanation, and this superiority to circumstance enchanted me. The most that was said was:

"The house is a little run down, you see."

Even this was said with such an air of satisfaction that I suspected my friends of not being saddened by the fact. Do you see a crew of bricklayers, carpenters, cabinet-workers, plasterers intruding their sacrilegious tools into so vivid a past, turning this in a week into a house you would never recognize, in which the family would feel that they were visiting strangers? A house without secrets, without recesses, without mysteries, without traps beneath the feet, or dungeons, a sort of town-hall reception room?

In a house with so many secret passages it was natural that the daughters should vanish before one's eyes. What must the attics be, when the drawing-room already contained all the wealth of an attic? When one could guess already that, the least cupboard opened, there would pour out sheaves of yellowed letters, grandpapa's receipted bills, more keys than there were locks and not one of which of course would fit any lock. Marvelously useless keys that confounded the reason and made it muse upon subterranean chambers, buried chests, treasures.

"Shall we go in to dinner?"

We went in to dinner. Moving from one room to the next I inhaled in passing that incense of an old library which is worth all the perfumes of the world. And particularly I liked the lamps being carried with us. Real lamps, heavy lamps, transported from room to room as in the time of my earliest childhood; stirring into motion as they passed great wondrous shadows on the walls. To pick one up was to displace bouquets of light and great black palms. Then, the lamps finally set down, there was a settling into motionlessness of the beaches of clarity and the vast reserves of surrounding darkness in which the wainscoting went on creaking.

As mysteriously and as silently as they had vanished, the girls reappeared. Gravely they took their places. Doubtless they had fed their dogs, their birds; had opened their windows on the bright night and breathed in the smell of the woods brought by the night wind. Now, unfolding their napkins, they were inspecting me cautiously out of the corners of their eyes, wondering whether or not they were going to make place for me among their domestic animals. For among others they had an iguana, a mongoose, a fox, a monkey, and bees. All these lived promiscuously together without quarreling in this new earthly paradise. The girls reigned over all the animals of creation, charming them with their little hands, feeding them, watering them, and telling them tales to which all, from mongoose to bees, gave ear.

I firmly expected that these alert young girls would employ all their critical faculty, all their shrewdness, in a swift, secret, and irrevocable judgment upon the male who sat opposite them.

When I was a child my sisters had a way of giving marks to guests who were honoring our table for the first time. Conversation might languish for a moment, and then in the silence we would hear the sudden impact of "Sixty!"—a word that could tickle only the family, who knew that one hundred was par. Branded by this low mark, the guest would all unknowing continue to spend himself in little courtesies while we sat screaming inwardly with delight.

Remembering that little game, I was worried. And it upset me a bit more to feel my judges so keen. Judges who knew how to distinguish between candid animals and animals that cheated; who could tell from the tracks of the fox whether he was in a good temper or not; whose instinct for inner movements was so sure and deep.

I liked the sharp eyes of these straightforward little souls, but I should so much have preferred that they play some other game. And yet, in my cowardly fear of their "sixty" I passed them the salt, poured out their wine; though each time that I raised my eyes I saw in their faces the gentle gravity of judges who were not to be bought.

Flattery itself was useless: they knew no vanity. Although they knew not it, they knew a marvelous pride, and without any help from me they thought more good of themselves than I should have dared utter. It did not even occur to me to draw any prestige from my craft, for it is extremely dangerous to clamber up to the topmost branches of a plane-tree simply to see if the nestlings are doing well or to say good morning to one's friends.

My taciturn young friends continued their inspection so imperturbably, I met so often their fleeting glances, that soon I stopped talking. Silence fell, and in that silence I heard something hiss faintly under the floor, rustle under the table, and then stop. I raised a pair of puzzled eyes. Thereupon, satisfied with her examination but applying her last touchstone, as she bit with savage young teeth into her bread the younger daughter explained to me with a candor by which she hoped to slaughter the barbarian (if that was what I was):

"It's the snakes."

And content, she said no more, as if that explanation should have sufficed for anyone in whom there remained a last glimmer of intelligence. Her sister sent a lightning glance to spy out my immediate reflex, and both bent with the gentlest and most ingenuous faces in the world over their plates.

"Ah! Snakes, are they?"

Naturally the words escaped from me against my will. This that had been gliding between my legs, had been brushing my calves, was snakes!

Fortunately for me, I smiled. Effortlessly. They would have known if it had been otherwise. I smiled because my heart was light, because each moment this house was more and more to my liking. And also because I wanted to know more about the snakes. The elder daughter came to my rescue.

"They nest in a hole under the table."

And her sister added: "They go back into their nest at about ten o'clock. During the day they hunt."

Now it was my turn to look at them out of the corner

of the eye. What shrewdness! what silent laughter behind those candid faces! And what sovereignty they
exercised, these princesses guarded by snakes! Princesses
for whom there existed no scorpion, no wasp, no serpent, but only little souls of animals!

As I write, I dream. All this is very far away. What
has become of these two fairy princesses? Girls so fine-
grained, so upright, have certainly attracted husbands.
Have they changed, I wonder? What do they do in
their new houses? Do they feel differently now about
the jungle growth and the snakes? They had been fused
with something universal, and then the day had come
when the woman had awakened in the maiden, when
there had surged in her a longing to find someone who
deserved a "Ninety-five." The dream of a ninety-five is
a weight on the heart.

And then an imbecile had come along. For the first
time those sharp eyes were mistaken and they dressed
him in gay colors. If the imbecile recited verse he was
thought a poet. Surely he must understand the holes in
the floor, must love the mongoose! The trust one put in
him, the swaying of the snakes between his legs under
the table—surely this must flatter him! And that heart
which was a wild garden was given to him who loved
only trim lawns. And the imbecile carried away the
princess into slavery.

· 7 ·

Men of the Desert

THESE, then, were some of the treasures that passed us by when for weeks and months and years we, pilots of the Sahara line, were prisoners of the sands, navigating from one stockade to the next with never an excursion outside the zone of silence. Oases like these did not prosper in the desert; these memories it dismissed as belonging to the domain of legend. No doubt there did gleam in distant places scattered round the world—places to which we should return once our work was done—there did gleam lighted windows. No doubt somewhere there did sit young girls among their white lemurs or their books, patiently compounding souls as rich in delight as secret gardens. No doubt there did exist such creatures waxing in beauty. But solitude cultivates a strange mood.

I know that mood. Three years of the desert taught it to me. Something in one's heart takes fright, not at the thought of growing old, not at feeling one's youth used up in this mineral universe, but at the thought that far away the whole world is ageing. The trees have brought forth their fruit; the grain has ripened in the fields; the women have bloomed in their loveliness. But the season is advancing and one must make haste; but the season is advancing and still one cannot leave; but the season is advancing . . . and other men will glean the harvest.

Many a night have I savored this taste of the irreparable, wandering in a circle round the fort, our prison, under the burden of the trade-winds. Sometimes, worn out by a day of flight, drenched in the humidity of the tropical climate, I have felt my heart beat in me like the wheels of an express train; and suddenly, more immediately than when flying, I have felt myself on a journey. A journey through time. Time was running through my fingers like the fine sand of the dunes; the poundings of my heart were bearing me onward towards an unknown future.

Ah, those fevers at night after a day of work in the silence! We seemed to ourselves to be burning up, like flares set out in the solitude.

And yet we knew joys we could not possibly have

known elsewhere. I shall never be able to express clearly whence comes this pleasure men take from aridity, but always and everywhere I have seen men attach themselves more stubbornly to barren lands than to any other. Men will die for a calcined, leafless, stony mountain. The nomads will defend to the death their great store of sand as if it were a treasure of gold dust. And we, my comrades and I, we too have loved the desert to the point of feeling that it was there we had lived the best years of our lives. I shall describe for you our stations (Port Etienne, Villa Cisneros, Cape Juby, were some of their names) and shall narrate for you a few of our days.

I

I succumbed to the desert as soon as I saw it, and I saw it almost as soon as I had won my wings. As early as the year 1926 I was transferred out of Europe to the Dakar-Juby division, where the Sahara meets the Atlantic and where, only recently, the Arabs had murdered two of our pilots, Erable and Gourp. In those days our planes frequently fell apart in mid-air, and because of this the African divisions were always flown by two ships, one without the mails trailing and convoying the other, prepared to take over the sacks in the event the mail plane broke down.

Under orders, I flew an empty ship down to Agadir. From Agadir I was flown to Dakar as a passenger, and it was on that flight that the vast sandy void and the mystery with which my imagination could not but endow it first thrilled me. But the heat was so intense that despite my excitement I dozed off soon after we left Port Etienne. Riguelle, who was flying me down, moved out to sea a couple of miles in order to get away from the sizzling surface of sand. I woke up, saw in the distance the thin white line of the coast, and said to myself fearfully that if anything went wrong we should surely drown. Then I dozed off again.

I was startled out of my sleep by a crash, a sudden silence, and then the voice of Riguelle saying, "Damn! There goes a connecting rod!" As I half rose out of my seat to send a regretful look at that white coast-line, now more precious than ever, he shouted to me angrily to stay as I was. I knew Riguelle had been wrong to go out to sea; I had been on the point of mentioning it; and now I felt a complete and savage satisfaction in our predicament. "This," I said to myself, "will teach him a lesson."

But this gratifying sense of superiority could obviously not last very long. Riguelle sent the plane earthward in a long diagonal line that brought us within sixty feet of the sand—an altitude at which there was no question of picking out a landing-place. We lost both wheels against one sand-dune, a wing against another, and crashed with a sudden jerk into a third.

"You hurt?" Riguelle called out.

"Not a bit," I said.

"That's what I call piloting a ship!" he boasted cheerfully.

I who was busy on all fours extricating myself from what had once been a ship, was in no mood to feed his pride.

"Guillaumet will be along in a minute to pick us up," he added.

Guillaumet was flying our convoy, and very shortly we saw him come down on a stretch of smooth sand a few hundred yards away. He asked if we were all right, was told no damage had been done, and then proposed briskly that we give him a hand with the sacks. The mail transferred out of the wrecked plane, they explained to me that in this soft sand it would not be possible to lift Guillaumet's plane clear if I was in it. They would hop to the next outpost, drop the mail there, and come back for me.

Now this was my first day in Africa. I was so ignorant that I could not tell a zone of danger from a zone of safety, I mean by that, a zone where the tribes had submitted peacefully to European rule from a zone where the tribes were still in rebellion. The region in which we had landed happened to be considered safe, but I did not know that.

"You've got a gun, of course," Riguelle said.

I had no gun and said so.

"My dear chap, you'll have to have a gun," he said,

and very kindly he gave me his. "And you'll want these extra clips of cartridges," he went on. "Just bear in mind that you shoot at anything and everything you see."

They had started to walk across to the other plane when Guillaumet, as if driven by his conscience, came back and handed me his cartridge clips, too. And with this they took off.

I was alone. They knew, though I did not, that I could have sat on one of these dunes for half a year without running the least danger. What they were doing was to implant in the imagination of a recruit a proper feeling of solitude and danger and respect with regard to their desert. What I was really feeling, however, was an immense pride. Sitting on the dune, I laid out beside me my gun and my five cartridge clips. For the first time since I was born it seemed to me that my life was my own and that I was responsible for it. Bear in mind that only two nights before I had been dining in a restaurant in Toulouse.

I walked to the top of a sand-hill and looked round the horizon like a captain on his bridge. This sea of sand bowled me over. Unquestionably it was filled with mystery and with danger. The silence that reigned over it was not the silence of emptiness but of plotting, of imminent enterprise. I sat still and stared into space. The end of the day was near. Something half revealed yet wholly unknown had bewitched me. The love of the

Sahara, like love itself, is born of a face perceived and never really seen. Ever after this first sight of your new love, an indefinable bond is established between you and the veneer of gold on the sand in the late sun.

Guillaumet's perfect landing broke the charm of my musings.

"Anything turn up?" he wanted to know.

I had seen my first gazelle. Silently it had come into view. I felt that the sands had shown me the gazelle in confidence, so I said nothing about it.

"You weren't frightened?"

I said no and thought, gazelles are not frightening.

The mails had been dropped at an outpost as isolated as an island in the Pacific. There, waiting for us, stood a colonial army sergeant. With his squad of fifteen black troops he stood guard on the threshold of the immense expanse. Every six months a caravan came up out of the desert and left him supplies.

Again and again he took our hands and looked into our eyes, ready to weep at the sight of us. "By God, I'm glad to see you! You don't know what it means to me to see you!" Only twice a year he saw a French face, and that was when, at the head of the camel corps, either the captain or the lieutenant came out of the inner desert.

We had to inspect his little fort—"built it with my own hands"—and swing his doors appreciatively—"as solid as they make 'em"—and drink a glass of wine with him.

"Another glass. Please! You don't know how glad I am to have some wine to offer you. Why, last time the captain came round I didn't have any for the captain. Think of that! I couldn't clink glasses with the captain and wish him luck! I was ashamed of myself. I asked to be relieved, I did!"

Clink glasses. Call out, "Here's luck!" to a man, running with sweat, who has just jumped down from the back of a camel. Wait six months for this great moment. Polish up your equipment. Scour the post from cellar to attic. Go up on the roof day after day and scan the horizon for that dust-cloud that serves as the envelope in which will be delivered to your door the Atar Camel Corps. And after all this, to have no wine in the house! To be unable to clink glasses. To see oneself dishonored.

"I keep waiting for the captain to come back," the sergeant said.

"Where is he, sergeant?"

And the sergeant, waving his arm in an arc that took in the whole horizon, said: "Nobody knows. Captain is everywhere at once."

We spent the night on the roof of the outpost, talking about the stars. There was nothing else in sight. All the stars were present, all accounted for, the way you see them from a plane, but fixed.

When the night is very fine and you are at the stick

of your ship, you half forget yourself and bit by bit the plane begins to tilt on the left. Pretty soon, while you still imagine yourself in plumb, you see the lights of a village under your right wing. There are no villages in the desert. A fishing-fleet in mid-ocean, then? There are no fishing-fleets in mid-Sahara. What—? Of course! You smile at the way your mind has wandered and you bring the ship back to plumb again. The village slips into place. You have hooked that particular constellation back in the panoply out of which it had fallen. Village? Yes, village of stars.

The sergeant had a word to say about them. "I know the stars," he said. "Steer by that star yonder and you make Tunis."

"Are you from Tunis?"

"No. My cousin, she is."

A long silence. But the sergeant could not keep anything back.

"I'm going to Tunis one of these days."

Not, I said to myself, by making a bee-line for that star and tramping across the desert; that is, not unless in the course of some raid a dried-up well should turn the sergeant over to the poetry of delirium. If that happened, star, cousin, and Tunis would melt into one, and the sergeant would certainly be off on that inspired tramp which the ignorant would think of as torture.

He went on. "I asked the captain for leave to go to Tunis, seeing my cousin is there and all. He said . . ."

"What did the captain say, sergeant?"

"Said: 'World's full of cousins.' Said: 'Dakar's nearer' and sent me there."

"Pretty girl, your cousin?"

"In Tunis? You bet! Blonde, she is."

"No, I mean at Dakar."

Sergeant, we could have hugged you for the wistful disappointed voice in which you answered, "She was a nigger."

II

Port Etienne is situated on the edge of one of the unsubdued regions of the Sahara. It is not a town. There is a stockade, a hangar, and a wooden quarters for the French crews. The desert all round is so unrelieved that despite its feeble military strength Port Etienne is practically invincible. To attack it means crossing such a belt of sand and flaming heat that the razzias (as the bands of armed marauders are called) must arrive exhausted and waterless. And yet, in the memory of man there has always been, somewhere in the North, a razzia marching on Port Etienne. Each time that the army captain who served as commandant of the fort came to drink a cup of tea with us, he would show us its route on the map the way a man might tell the legend of a beautiful princess.

But the razzia never arrived. Like a river, it was each time dried up by the sands, and we called it the phantom razzia. The cartridges and hand grenades that the government passed out to us nightly would sleep peacefully in their boxes at the foot of our beds. Our surest protection was our poverty, our single enemy silence. Night and day, Lucas, who was chief of the airport, would wind his gramophone; and Ravel's *Bolero*, flung up here so far out of the path of life, would speak to us in a half-lost language, provoking an aimless melancholy which curiously resembled thirst.

One evening we had dined at the fort and the commandant had shown off his garden to us. Someone had sent him from France, three thousand miles away, a few boxes of real soil, and out of this soil grew three green leaves which we caressed as if they had been jewels. The commandant would say of them, "This is my park." And when there arose one of those sand-storms that shriveled everything up, he would move the park down into the cellar.

Our quarters stood about a mile from the fort, and after dinner we walked home in the moonlight. Under the moon the sands were rosy. We were conscious of our destitution, but the sands were rosy. A sentry called out, and the pathos of our world was re-established. The whole of the Sahara lay in fear of our shadows and called for the password, for a razzia was on the march. All the voices of the desert resounded in that sentry's challenge. No longer was the desert an empty prison: a Moorish caravan had magnetized the night.

We might believe ourselves secure, and yet, illness,

accident, razzia—how many dangers were afoot! Man inhabits the earth, a target for secret marksmen. The Senegalese sentry was there like a prophet of old to remind us of our destiny. We gave the password, *Français!* and passed before the black angel. Once in quarters, we breathed more freely. With what nobility that threat had endowed us! Oh, distant it still was, and so little urgent, deadened by so much sand; but yet the world was no longer the same. Once again this desert had become a sumptuous thing. A razzia that was somewhere on the march, yet never arrived, was the source of its glory.

It was now eleven at night. Lucas came back from the wireless and told me that the plane from Dakar would be in at midnight. All well on board. By ten minutes past midnight the mails would be transferred to my ship and I should take off for the North. I shaved carefully in a cracked mirror. From time to time, a Turkish towel hanging at my throat, I went to the door and looked at the naked sand. The night was fine but the wind was dropping. I went back again to the mirror. I was thoughtful.

A wind that has been running for months and then drops sometimes fouls the entire sky. I got into my harness, snapped my emergency lamps to my belt along with my altimeter and my pencils. I went over to Néri, who was to be my radio operator on this flight. He was shaving too. I said, "Everything all right?" For the moment everything was all right. But I heard something sizzling. It was a dragonfly knocking against the lamp. Why it was I cannot say, but I felt a twinge in my heart.

I went out of doors and looked round. The air was pure. A cliff on the edge of the airdrome stood in profile against the sky as if it were daylight. Over the desert reigned a vast silence as of a house in order. But here were a green butterfly and two dragonflies knocking against my lamp. And again I felt a dull ache which might as easily have been joy as fear but came up from the depths of me, so vague that it could scarcely be said to be there. Someone was calling to me from a great distance. Was it instinct?

Once again I went out. The wind had died down completely. The air was still cool. But I had received a warning. I guessed, I believed I could guess, what I was expecting. Was I right? Neither the sky nor the sand had made the least sign to me; but two dragonflies and a moth had spoken.

I climbed a dune and sat down face to the east. If I was right, the thing would not be long coming. What were they after here, those dragonflies, hundreds of miles from their oases inland? Wreckage thrown up on the strand bears witness to a storm at sea. Even so did these insects declare to me that a sand-storm was on the way, a storm out of the east that had blown them out of their oases.

Solemnly, for it was fraught with danger, the east wind rose. Already its foam had touched me. I was the extreme edge lapped by the wave. Fifty feet behind me no sail would have flapped. Its flame wrapped me round once, only once, in a caress that seemed dead. But I knew, in the seconds that followed, that the Sahara was catching its breath and would send forth a second sigh. And that before three minutes had passed the air-sock of our hangar would be whipped into action. And that before ten minutes had gone by the sand would fill the air. We should shortly be taking off in this conflagration, in this return of the flames from the desert.

But that was not what excited me. What filled me with a barbaric joy was that I had understood a murmured monosyllable of this secret language, had sniffed the air and known what was coming, like one of those primitive men to whom the future is revealed in such faint rustlings; it was that I had been able to read the anger of the desert in the beating wings of a dragonfly.

III

But we were not always in the air, and our idle hours were spent taming the Moors. They would come out of their forbidden regions (those regions we crossed in our flights and where they would shoot at us the whole length of our crossing), would venture to the stockade in the hope of buying loaves of sugar, cotton cloth, tea, and then would sink back again into their mystery. Whenever they turned up we would try to tame a few of them in order to establish little nuclei of friendship in the desert; thus if we were forced down among them there would be at any rate a few who might be persuaded to sell us into slavery rather than massacre us.

Now and then an influential chief came up, and him, with the approval of the Line, we would load into the plane and carry off to see something of the world. The aim was to soften their pride, for, repositories of the truth, defenders of Allah, the only God, it was more in contempt than in hatred that he and his kind murdered their prisoners.

When they met us in the region of Juby or Cisneros, they never troubled to shout abuse at us. They would merely turn away and spit; and this not by way of personal insult but out of sincere disgust at having crossed the path of a Christian. Their pride was born of the illusion of their power. Allah renders a believer invincible. Many a time a chief has said to me, pointing to his army of three hundred rifles, "Lucky it is for France that she lies more than a hundred days' march from here."

And so we would take them up for a little spin. Three of them even visited France in our planes. I happened to be present when they returned. I met them when they landed, went with them to their tents, and waited in infinite curiosity to hear their first words. They were of the same race as those who, having once been flown by me to the Senegal, had burst into tears at the sight of trees. What a revelation Europe must have been for them! And yet their first replies astonished me by their coolness.

"Paris? Very big."

Everything was "very big"—Paris, the Trocadéro, the automobiles.

What with everyone in Paris asking if the Louvre was not "very big" they had gradually learned that this was the answer that flattered us. And with a sort of vague contempt, as if pacifying a lot of children, they would grant that the Louvre was "very big."

These Moors took very little trouble to dissemble the freezing indifference they felt for the Eiffel Tower, the steamships, and the locomotives. They were ready to agree once and for always that we knew how to build things out of iron. We also knew how to fling a bridge from one continent to another. The plain fact was that they did not know enough to admire our technical progress. The wireless astonished them less than the telephone, since the mystery of the telephone resided in the very fact of the wire.

It took a little time for me to understand that my questions were on the wrong track. For what they thought admirable was not the locomotive, but the tree. When you think of it, a tree does possess a perfection that a locomotive cannot know. And then I remembered the Moors who had wept at the sight of trees.

Yes, France was in some sense admirable, but it was not because of those stupid things made of iron. They had seen pastures in France in which all the camels of Er-Reguibat could have grazed! There were forests in France! The French had cows, cows filled with milk! And of course my three Moors were amazed by the incredible customs of the people.

"In Paris," they said, "you walk through a crowd of a thousand people. You stare at them. And nobody carries a rifle!"

But there were better things in France than this inconceivable friendliness between men. There was the circus, for example.

"Frenchwomen," they said, "can jump standing from one galloping horse to another."

Thereupon they would stop and reflect.

"You take one Moor from each tribe," they went on. "You take him to the circus. And nevermore will the tribes of Er-Reguibat make war on the French."

I remember my chiefs sitting among the crowding tribesmen in the opening of their tents, savoring the pleasure of reciting this new series of Arabian Nights, extolling the music halls in which naked women dance on carpets of flowers.

Here were men who had never seen a tree, a river, a rose; who knew only through the Koran of the existence of gardens where streams run, which is their name for Paradise. In their desert, Paradise and its beautiful captives could be won only by bitter death from an infidel's rifle-shot, after thirty years of a miserable existence. But God had tricked them, since from the Frenchmen to whom he grants these treasures he exacts payment neither by thirst nor by death. And it was upon this that the chiefs now mused. This was why, gazing out at the Sahara surrounding their tents, at that desert with its barren promise of such thin pleasures, they let themselves go in murmured confidences.

"You know . . . the God of the French . . . He is more generous to the French than the God of the Moors is to the Moors."

Memories that moved them too deeply rose to stop their speech. Some weeks earlier they had been taken up into the French Alps. Here in Africa they were still dreaming of what they saw. Their guide had led them to a tremendous waterfall, a sort of braided column roaring over the rocks. He had said to them:

"Taste this."

It was sweet water. Water! How many days were they wont to march in the desert to reach the nearest well; and when they had arrived, how long they had to dig before there bubbled a muddy liquid mixed with camel's urine! Water! At Cape Juby, at Cisneros, at Port Etienne, the Moorish children did not beg for coins. With empty tins in their hands they begged for water.

"Give me a little water, give!"

"If you are a good lad . . ."

Water! A thing worth its weight in gold! A thing the least drop of which drew from the sand the green sparkle of a blade of grass! When rain has fallen anywhere, a great exodus animates the Sahara. The tribes ride towards that grass that will have sprung up two hundred miles away. And this water, this miserly water of which not a drop had fallen at Port Etienne in ten years, roared in the Savoie with the power of a cataclysm as if, from some burst cistern, the reserves of the world were pouring forth.

"Come, let us leave," their guide had said.

But they would not stir.

"Leave us here a little longer."

They had stood in silence. Mute, solemn, they had stood gazing at the unfolding of a ceremonial mystery. That which came roaring out of the belly of the mountain was life itself, was the life-blood of man. The flow of a single second would have resuscitated whole caravans that, mad with thirst, had pressed on into the eternity of salt lakes and mirages. Here God was manifesting Himself: it would not do to turn one's back on Him. God had opened the locks and was displaying His puissance. The three Moors had stood motionless.

"That is all there is to see," their guide had said.
"Come."

"We must wait,"

"Wait for what?"

"The end."

They were awaiting the moment when God would
grow weary of His madness. They knew Him to be
quick to repent, knew He was miserly.

"But that water has been running for a thousand
years!"

And this was why, at Port Etienne, they did not too
strongly stress the matter of the waterfall. There were
certain miracles about which it was better to be silent.
Better, indeed, not to think too much about them, for
in that case one would cease to understand anything at
all. Unless one was to doubt the existence of God. . . .

"You see . . . the God of the Frenchmen . . ."

But I knew them well, my barbarians. There they
sat, perplexed in their faith, disconcerted, and henceforth quite ready to acknowledge French overlordship.
They were dreaming of being victualed in barley by
the French administration, and assured of their security
by our Saharan regiments. There was no question but
that they would, by their submission, be materially better off.

But all three were of the blood of el Mammun.

I had known el Mammun when he was our vassal.

Loaded with official honors for services rendered, enriched by the French Government and respected by the tribes, he seemed to lack for nothing that belonged to the state of an Arab prince. And yet one night, without a sign of warning, he had massacred all the French officers in his train, had seized camels and rifles, and had fled to rejoin the refractory tribes in the interior.

Treason is the name given to these sudden uprisings, these flights at once heroic and despairing of a chieftain henceforth proscribed in the desert, this brief glory that will go out like a rocket against the low wall of European carbines. This sudden madness is properly a subject for amazement.

And yet the story of el Mammun was that of many other Arab chiefs. He grew old. Growing old, one begins to ponder. Pondering thus, el Mammun discovered one night that he had betrayed the God of Islam and had sullied his hand by sealing in the hand of the Christians a pact in which he had been stripped of everything.

Indeed what were barley and peace to him? A warrior disgraced and become a shepherd, he remembered a time when he had inhabited a Sahara where each fold in the sands was rich with hidden mysteries; where forward in the night the tip of the encampment was studded with sentries; where the news that spread concerning the movements of the enemy made all hearts beat faster round the night fires. He remembered a taste of the high seas which, once savored by man, is never forgotten. And because of his pact he was condemned to wander without glory through a region pacified and voided of all prestige. Then, truly and for the first time, the Sahara became a desert.

It is possible that he was fond of the officers he murdered. But love of Allah takes precedence.

"Good night, el Mammun."

"God guard thee!"

The officers rolled themselves up in their blankets and stretched out upon the sand as on a raft, face to the stars. High overhead all the heavens were wheeling slowly, a whole sky marking the hour. There was the moon, bending towards the sands, and the Frenchmen, lured by her tranquillity into oblivion, fell asleep. A few minutes more, and only the stars gleamed. And then, in order that the corrupted tribes be regenerated into their past splendor, in order that there begin again those flights without which the sands would have no radiance, it was enough that these Christians drowned in their slumber send forth a feeble wail. Still a few seconds more, and from the irreparable will come forth an empire.

And the handsome sleeping lieutenants were massacred.

IV

Today at Cape Juby, Kemal and his brother Mouyan have invited me to their tent. I sit drinking tea while Mouyan stares at me in silence. Blue sandveil drawn across his mouth, he maintains an unsociable reserve. Kemal alone speaks to me and does the honors:

"My tent, my camels, my wives, my slaves are yours."

Mouyan, his eyes still fixed on me, bends towards his brother, pronounces a few words, and lapses into silence again.

"What does he say?" I ask.

"He says that Bonnafous has stolen a thousand camels from the tribes of Er-Reguibat."

I have never met this Captain Bonnafous, but I know that he is an officer of the camel corps garrisoned at Atar and I have gathered from the Moors that to them he is a legendary figure. They speak of him with anger, but as of a sort of god. His presence lends price to the sand. Now once again, no one knows how, he has out-flanked the southward marching razzias, taken them in the rear, driven off their camels by the hundred, and forced them to turn about and pursue him unless they are to lose those treasures which they had thought se-cure. And now, having saved Atar by this archangelic irruption and planted his camp upon a high limestone plateau, he stands there like a guerdon to be won, and such is his magnetism that the tribes are obliged to march towards his sword.

With a hard look at me, Mouyan speaks again.

"What now?" I ask.

"He says we are off tomorrow on a razzia against Bonnafous. Three hundred rifles."

I had guessed something of the sort. These camels led to the wells for three days past; these powwows; this fever running through the camp: it was as if men had been rigging an invisible ship. Already the air was filled with the wind that would take her out of port. Thanks to Bonnafous, each step to the South was to be a noble step rich in honor. It has become impossible to say whether love or hate plays the greater part in this setting forth of the warriors.

There is something magnificent in the possession of an enemy of Bonnafous' mettle. Where he turns up, the near-by tribes fold their tents, collect their camels and fly, trembling to think they might have found themselves face to face with him; while the more distant tribes are seized by a vertigo resembling love. They tear themselves from the peace of their tents, from the embraces of their women, from the happiness of slumber, for suddenly there is nothing in the world that can match in beauty, after two months of exhausting march, of burning thirst, of halts crouching under the sandstorm, the joy of falling unexpectedly at dawn upon the Atar camel corps and there, God willing, killing Captain Bonnafous.

"Bonnafous is very clever," Kemal avows.

Now I know their secret. Even as men who desire a woman dream of her indifferent footfall, toss and turn in the night, scorched and wounded by the indifference of that stroll she takes through their dream, so the distant progress of Bonnafous torments these warriors.

This Christian in Moorish dress at the head of his two hundred marauding cameleers, Moors themselves, outflanking the razzias hurled against him, has marched boldly into the country of the refractory tents where the least of his own men, freed from the constraint of the garrison, might with impunity shake off his servitude and sacrifice the captain to his God on the stony table-lands. He has gone into a world where only his prestige restrains his men, where his weakness itself is the cause of their dread. And tonight, through their raucous slumber he strolls to and fro with heedless step, and his footfall resounds in the innermost heart of the desert.

Mouyan ponders, still motionless against the back wall of the tent, like a block of blue granite cut in low relief. Only his eyes gleam, and his silver knife has ceased to be a plaything. I have the feeling that since becoming part of a razzia he has entered into a different world. To him the dunes are alive. The wind is charged with odors. He senses as never before his own nobility and crushes me beneath his contempt; for he is to ride against Bonnafous, he is to move at dawn impelled by a hatred that bears all the signs of love.

Once again he leans towards his brother, whispers, and stares at me.

"What is he saying?" I ask once again.

"That he will shoot you if he meets you outside the fort."

"Why?"

"He says you have airplanes and the wireless; you have Bonnafous; but you have not the Truth."

Motionless in the sculptured folds of his blue cloak, Mouyan has judged me.

"He says you eat greens like the goat and pork like the pigs. Your wives are shameless and show their faces —he has seen them. He says you never pray. He says, what good are your airplanes and wireless and Bonnafous, if you do not possess the Truth?"

And I am forced to admire this Moor who is not about to defend his freedom, for in the desert a man is always free; who is not about to defend his visible treasures, for the desert is bare; but who is about to defend a secret kingdom.

In the silence of the sand-waves Bonnafous leads his troop like a corsair of old; by the grace of Bonnafous the oasis of Cape Juby has ceased to be a haunt of idle shepherds and has become something as signal, as portentous, as admirable as a ship on the high seas. Bonnafous is a storm beating against the ship's side, and because of him the tent cloths are closed at night. How poignant is the southern silence! It is Bonnafous' silence. Mouyan, that old hunter, listens to his footfall in the wind.

When Bonnafous returns to France his enemies, far

from rejoicing, will bewail his absence, as if his departure had deprived the desert of one of its magnetic poles and their existence of a part of its prestige. They will say to me:

"Why does Bonnafous leave us?"

"I do not know."

For years he had accepted their rules as his rules. He had staked his life against theirs. He had slept with his head pillowed on their rocks. Like them he had known Biblical nights of stars and wind in the course of the ceaseless pursuit. And of a sudden he proves to them, by the fact of leaving the desert, that he has not been gambling for a stake he deemed essential. Unconcernedly, he throws in his hand and rises from the table. And those Moors he leaves at their gambling lose confidence in the significance of a game which does not involve this man to the last drop of his blood. Still, they try to believe in him:

"Your Bonnafous will come back."

"I do not know."

He will come back, they tell themselves. The games of Europe will never satisfy him—garrison bridge, promotion, women, and the rest. Haunted by his lost honor he will come back to this land where each step makes the heart beat faster like a step towards love or towards death. He had imagined that the Sahara was a mere adventure and that what was essential in life lay in Europe; but he will discover with disgust that it was here in the desert he possessed his veritable treasures—this prestige of the sand, the night, the silence, this homeland of wind and stars.

And if Bonnafous should come back one day, the news will spread in a single night throughout the country of the refractory tribes. The Moors will know that somewhere in the Sahara, at the head of his two hundred marauders, Bonnafous is again on the march. They will lead their dromedaries in silence to the wells. They will prepare their provisions of barley. They will clean and oil their breech-loaders, impelled by a hatred that partakes of love.

V

"Hide me in the Marrakech plane!"

Night after night, at Cape Juby, this slave would make his prayer to me. After which, satisfied that he had done what he could for his salvation, he would sit down upon crossed legs and brew my tea. Having put himself in the hands of the only doctor (as he believed) who could cure him, having prayed to the only god who might save him, he was at peace for another twenty-four hours.

Squatting over his kettle, he would summon up the simple vision of his past—the black earth of Marrakech, the pink houses, the rudimentary possessions of which he had been despoiled. He bore me no ill-will for my silence, nor for my delay in restoring him to life. I was not a man like himself but a power to be invoked, something like a favorable wind which one of these days might smile upon his destiny.

I, for my part, did not labor under these delusions concerning my power. What was I but a simple pilot, serving my few months as chief of the airport at Cape Juby and living in a wooden hut built over against the Spanish fort, where my worldly goods consisted of a basin, a jug of brackish water, and a cot too short for me?

"We shall see, Bark."

All slaves are called Bark, so Bark was his name. But despite four years of captivity he could not resign himself to it and remembered constantly that he had been a king.

"What did you do at Marrakech, Bark?"

At Marrakech, where his wife and three children were doubtless still living, he had plied a wonderful trade.

"I was a drover, and my name was Mohammed!"

The very magistrates themselves would send for him.

"Mohammed, I have some steers to sell. Go up into the mountains and bring them down."

Or:

"I have a thousand sheep in the plain. Lead them up into the higher pastures."

And Bark, armed with an olive-wood sceptre, governed their exodus. He and no other held sway over the nation of ewes, restrained the liveliest because of the lambkins about to be born, stirred up the laggards, strode forward in a universe of confidence and obedience. Nobody but him could say where lay the promised land towards which he led his flock. He alone could read his way in the stars, for the science he possessed was not shared by the sheep. Only he, in his wisdom, decided when they should take their rest, when they should drink at the springs. And at night while they slept, Bark, physician and prophet and king, standing in wool to the knees and swollen with tenderness for so much feeble ignorance, would pray for his people.

One day he was stopped by some Arabs.

"Come with us to fetch cattle up from the South," they said.

They had walked him a long time, and when, after three days, they found themselves deep in the mountains, on the borders of rebellion, the Arabs had quietly placed a hand on his shoulder, christened him Bark, and sold him into slavery.

He was not the only slave I knew. I used to go daily to the tents to take tea. Stretched out with naked feet on the thick woolen carpet which is the nomad's luxury and upon which for a time each day he builds his house, I would taste the happiness of the journeying hours. In the desert, as on shipboard, one is sensible of the passage of time. In that parching heat a man feels that the day is

a voyage towards the goal of evening, towards the promise of a cool breeze that will bathe the limbs and wash
away the sweat. Under the heat of the day beasts and
men plod towards the sweet well of night as confidently
as towards death. Thus, idleness here is never vain; and
each day seems as comforting as the roads that lead to
the sea.

I knew the slaves well. They would come in as soon
as the chief had taken out the little stove, the kettle, and
the glasses from his treasure chest—that chest heavy with
absurd objects, with locks lacking keys, vases for
non-existent flowers, threepenny mirrors, old weapons,
things so disparate that they might have been salvaged
from a ship cast up here in the desert.

Then the mute slave would cram the stove with twigs,
blow on the embers, fill the kettle with water, and in
this service that a child could perform, set into motion
a play of muscles able to uproot a tree.

I would wonder what he was thinking of, and would
sense that he was at peace with himself. There was no
doubt that he was hypnotized by the motions he went
through—brewing tea, tending the camels, eating. Under
the blistering day he walked towards the night; and
under the ice of the naked stars he longed for the return
of day. Happy are the lands of the North whose seasons
are poets, the summer composing a legend of snow, the
winter a tale of sun. Sad the tropics, where in the sweat-
ing-room nothing changes very much. But happy also

the Sahara where day and night swing man so evenly from one hope to the other.

Tea served, the black will squat outside the tent, relishing the evening wind. In this sluggish captive hulk, memories have ceased to swarm. Even the moment when he was carried off is faint in his mind—the blows, the shouts, the arms of men that brought him down into his present night. And since that hour he has sunk deeper and deeper into a queer slumber, divested like a blind man of his Senegalese rivers or his white Moroccan towns, like a deaf man of the sound of familiar voices.

This black is not unhappy; he is crippled. Dropped down one day into the cycle of desert life, bound to the nomadic migrations, chained for life to the orbits they describe in the sand, how could he retain any memory of a past, a home, a wife and children, all of them for him as dead as the dead?

Men who have lived for years with a great love, and have lived on in noble solitude when it was taken from them, are likely now and then to be worn out by their exaltation. Such men return humbly to a humdrum life, ready to accept contentment in a more commonplace love. They find it sweet to abdicate, to resign themselves to a kind of servility and to enter into the peace of things. This black is proud of his master's embers.

Like a ship moving into port, we of the desert come up into the night. In this hour, because it is the hour when all the weariness of day is remitted and its heats have ceased, when master and slave enter side by side into the cool of evening, the master is kind to the slave.

"Here, take this," the chief says to the captive.

He allows him a glass of tea. And the captive, over-come with gratitude for a glass of tea, would kiss his master's knees. This man before me is not weighed down with chains. How little need he has of them! How faithful he is! How submissively he forswears the deposed king within him! Truly, the man is a mere contented slave.

And yet the day will come when he will be set free. When he has grown too old to be worth his food or his cloak, he will be inconceivably free. For three days he will offer himself in vain from tent to tent, growing each day weaker; until towards the end of the third day, still uncomplaining, he will lie down on the sand.

I have seen them die naked like this at Cape Juby. The Moors jostle their long death-struggle, though with-out ill intent; and the children play in the vicinity of the dark wreck, running with each dawn to see if it is still stirring, yet without mocking the old servitor. It is all in the nature of things. It is as if they had said to him: "You have done a good day's work and have the right to sleep. Go to bed."

And the old slave, still outstretched, suffers hunger which is but vertigo, and not injustice which alone is torment. Bit by bit he becomes one with the earth, is shriveled up by the sun and received by the earth.

Thirty years of toil, and then this right to slumber and to the earth.

The first one I saw did not moan; but then he had no one to moan against. I felt in him an obscure acquiescence, as of a mountaineer lost and at the end of his strength who sinks to earth and wraps himself up in dreams and snow. What was painful to me was not his suffering (for I did not believe he was suffering); it was that for the first time it came on me that when a man dies, an unknown world passes away.

I could not tell what visions were vanishing in the dying slave, what Senegalese plantations or white Moroccan towns. It was impossible for me to know whether, in this black heap, there was being extinguished merely a world of petty cares in the breast of a slave— the tea to be brewed, the camels watered; or whether, revived by a surge of memories, a man lay dying in the glory of humanity. The hard bone of his skull was in a sense an old treasure chest; and I could not know what colored stuffs, what images of festivities, what vestiges, obsolete and vain in this desert, had here escaped the shipwreck.

The chest was there, locked and heavy. I could not know what bit of the world was crumbling in this man during the gigantic slumber of his ultimate days, was disintegrating in this consciousness and this flesh which little by little was reverting to night and to root.

"I was a drover, and my name was Mohammed!"

Before I met Bark I had never met a slave who offered the least resistance. That the Moors had violated his freedom, had in a single day stripped him as naked as a newborn infant, was not the point. God sometimes sends cyclones which in a single hour wipe out a man's harvests. But deeper than his belongings, these Moors had threatened him in his very essence.

Many another captive would have resigned himself to the death in him of the poor herdsman who toiled the year round for a crust of bread. Not so Bark. He refused to settle into a life of servitude, to surrender to the weariness of waiting and resign himself to a passive contentment. He rejected the slave-joys that are contingent upon the kindness of the slave-owner. Within his breast Mohammed absent held fast to the house Mohammed had lived in. That house was sad for being empty, but none other should live in it. Bark was like one of those white-haired caretakers who die of their fidelity in the weeds of the paths and the tedium of silence.

He never said, "I am Mohammed ben Lhaoussin"; he said, "My name was Mohammed," dreaming of the day when that obliterated figure would again live within him in all its glory and by the power of its resuscitation would drive out the ghost of the slave.

There were times when, in the silence of the night, all his memories swept over him with the poignancy of a song of childhood. Our Arab interpreter said to me, "In the middle of the night he woke up and talked about Marrakech; and he wept." No man in solitude can escape these recurrences. The old Mohammed awoke in him without warning, stretched himself in his limbs, sought his wife against his flank in this desert where no woman had ever approached Bark, and listened to the water purling in the fountains here where no fountain ran.

And Bark, his eyes shut, sitting every night under the same star, in a place where men live in houses of hair and follow the wind, told himself that he was living in his white house in Marrakech. His body charged with tenderness and mysteriously magnetized, as if the pole of these emotions were very near at hand, Bark would come to see me. He was trying to let me know that he was ready, that his over-full heart was quivering on the brim and needed only to find itself back in Marrakech to be poured out. And all that was wanted was a sign from me. Bark would smile, would whisper to me how it could be done—for of course I should not have thought of this dodge:

"The mails leave tomorrow. You stow me away in the Marrakech plane."

"Poor old Bark!"

We were stationed among the unsubdued tribes, and how could we help him away? God knows what massacre the Moors would have done among us that very day to avenge the insult of this theft. I had, indeed, tried

to buy him, with the help of the mechanics at the port—
Laubergue, Marchal, and Abgrall. But it was not every
day that the Moors met Europeans in quest of a slave,
and they took advantage of the occasion.

"Twenty thousand francs."

"Don't make me laugh!"

"But look at those strong arms. . . ."

Months passed before the Moors came down to a
reasonable figure and I, with the help of friends at home
to whom I had written, found myself in a position to
buy old Bark. There was a week of bargaining which
we spent, fifteen Moors and I, sitting in a circle in the
sand. A friend of Bark's master who was also my friend,
Zin Ould Rhattari, a bandit, was privately on my side.

"Sell him," he would argue in accordance with my
coaching. "You will lose him one of these days, you
know. Bark is a sick man. He is diseased. You can't see
yet, but he is sick inside. One of these days he will swell
right up. Sell him as soon as you can to the Frenchman."

I had promised fifty Spanish pesetas to another bandit,
Raggi, and Raggi would say:

"With the money you get for Bark you will be able
to buy camels and rifles and cartridges. Then you can
go off on a razzia against these French. Go down to
Atar and bring back three or four young Senegalese.
Get rid of the old carcass."

And so Bark was sold to me. I locked him up for six

days in our hut, for if he had wandered out before the arrival of a plane the Moors would surely have kidnapped him. Meanwhile, although I would not allow him out, I set him free with a flourish of ceremony in the presence of three Moorish witnesses. One was a local marabout, another was Ibrahim, the mayor of Cape Juby, and the third was his former owner. These three pirates, who would gladly have cut off Bark's head within fifty feet of the fort for the sole pleasure of doing me in the eye, embraced him warmly and signed the official act of manumission. That done, they said to him:

"You are now our son."

He was my son, too, by law. Dutifully, Bark embraced all his fathers.

He lived on in our hut in comfortable captivity until we could ship him home. Over and over again, twenty times a day, he would ask to have the simple journey described. We were flying him to Agadir. There he would be given an omnibus ticket to Marrakech. He was to be sure not to miss the bus. That was all there was to it. But Bark played at being free the way a child plays at being an explorer, going over and over this journey back to life—the bus, the crowds, the towns he would pass through.

One day Laubergue came to talk to me about Bark. He said that Marchal and Abgrall and he rather felt it would be a shame if Bark was flung into the world without a copper. They had made up a purse of a thousand francs: didn't I think that would see Bark through till he found work? I thought of all the old ladies who run charities and insist upon gratitude in exchange for every twenty francs they part with. These airplane mechanics were parting with a thousand francs, had no thought of charity, and were even less concerned about gratitude.

Nor were they acting out of pity, like those old ladies who want to believe they are spreading happiness. They were contributing simply to restore to a man his lost dignity as a human being. They knew quite as well as anybody else that once the initial intoxication of his homecoming was past, the first faithful friend to step up and take Bark's hand would be Poverty; and that before three months had gone by he would be tearing up sleepers somewhere on the railway line for a living. He was sure to be less well off there than here in the desert. But in their view he had the right to live his life among his own people.

"Good-by, old Bark. Be a man!"

The plane quivered, ready to take off. Bark took his last look at the immense desolation of Cape Juby. Round the plane two hundred Moors were finding out what a slave looked like when he stood on the threshold of life. They would make no bones about snatching him back again if a little later the ship happened to be forced down.

We stood about our fifty-year-old, new-born babe, worried a little at having launched him forth on the stream of life.

"Good-by, Bark!"

"No!"

"What do you mean?"

"No. I am Mohammed ben Lhaoussin."

The last news we had of him was brought back to us by Abdullah who at our request had looked after Bark at Agadir. The plane reached Agadir in the morning, but the bus did not leave until evening. This was how Bark spent his day.

He began by wandering through the town and remaining silent so long that his restlessness upset Abdullah.

"Anything the matter?"

"No."

This freedom had come too suddenly: Bark was finding it hard to orient himself. There was a vague happiness in him, but with this exception there was scarcely any difference between the Bark of yesterday and the Bark of today. Yet he had as much right to the sun, henceforth, as other men; as much right as they to sit in the shade of an Arab café.

He sat down and ordered tea for Abdullah and himself. This was his first lordly gesture, a manifestation of a power that ought to have transfigured him in other men's eyes. But the waiter poured his tea quite without surprise, quite unaware that in this gesture he was doing homage to a free man.

"Let us go somewhere else," Bark had said; and they had gone off to the Kasbah, the licensed quarter of the town. The little Berber prostitutes came up and greeted them, so kind and tame that here Bark felt he might be coming alive.

These girls were welcoming a man back to life, but they knew nothing of this. They took him by the hand, offered him tea, then love, very nicely; but exactly as they would have offered it to any man. Bark, preoccupied with his message, tried to tell them the story of his resurrection. They smiled most sympathetically. They were glad for him, since he was glad. And to make the wonder more wonderful he added, "I am Mohammed ben Lhaoussin."

But that was no surprise to them. All men have names, and so many return from afar! They could guess, nevertheless, that this man had suffered, and they strove to be as gentle as possible with the poor black devil. He appreciated their gentleness, this first gift that life was making him; but his restlessness was yet not stilled. He had not yet rediscovered his empire.

Back to town went Bark and Abdullah. He idled in front of the Jewish shops, stared at the sea, repeated to himself that he could walk as he pleased in any direction, that he was free. But this freedom had in it a taste of bitterness: what he learned from it with most intensity was that he had no ties with the world.

At that moment a child had come up. Bark stroked the soft cheek. The child smiled. This was not one of the master's children that one had to flatter. It was a sickly child whose cheek Bark was stroking. And the child was smiling at him. The child awoke something in Bark, and Bark felt himself more important on earth because of the sickly child whose smile was his due. He began to sense confusedly that something was stirring within him, was striding forward with swift steps.

"What are you looking for?" Abdullah had asked him.

"Nothing," was again Bark's answer.

But when, rounding a corner, he came upon a group of children at play, he stopped. This was it. He stared at them in silence. Then he went off to the Jewish shops and came back laden with treasure. Abdullah was nettled:

"Fool! Throwing away your money!"

Bark gave no heed. Solemnly he beckoned to each child in turn, and the little hands rose towards the toys and the bangles and the gold-sewn slippers. Each child, as soon as he had a firm grip on his treasure, fled like a wild thing, and Bark went back to the Jewish shops.

Other children in Agadir, hearing the news, ran after him; and these too were shod by Bark in golden slippers. The tale spread to the outskirts of Agadir, whence still other children scurried into town and clustered round the black god, clinging to his threadbare cloak and clamoring for their due. Bark, that victim of a sombre joy, spent on them his last copper.

Abdullah was sure that he had gone mad, "mad with joy," he said afterward. But I incline to believe that Bark was not sharing with others an overflow of happiness. He was free, and therefore he possessed the essential of wealth—the right to the love of Berber girls, to go north or south as he pleased, to earn his bread by his toil. What good was this money when the thing for which he was famished was to be a man in the family of men, bound by ties to other men?

The town prostitutes had been kind to old Bark, but he had been able to get away from them as easily as he had come to them: they had no need of him. The waiter in the café, the passers-by in the streets, the shopkeepers, had respected the free man he was, sharing their sun with him on terms of equality; but none of them had indicated that he needed Bark.

He was free, but too infinitely free; not striding upon the earth but floating above it. He felt the lack in him of that weight of human relations that trammels a man's progress; tears, farewells, reproaches, joys—all those things that a man caresses or rips apart each time he sketches a gesture; those thousand ties that bind him to others and lend density to his being. But already Bark was in ballast of a thousand hopes.

And so the reign of Bark began in the glory of the sun setting over Agadir, in that evening coolness that so long had been for him the single sweetness, the unique stall in which he could take his rest. And as the hour of leaving approached, Bark went forward lapped in this tide of children as once in his sea of ewes, ploughing his first furrow in the world. He would go back next day to the poverty of his family, to responsibility for more lives than perhaps his old arms would be able to sustain; but already, among these children, he felt the pull of his true weight. Like an archangel too airy to live the life of man, but who had cheated, had sewn lead into his girdle, Bark dragged himself forward, pulling against the pull of a thousand children who had such great need of golden slippers.

Such is the desert. A Koran which is but a handbook of the rules of the game transforms its sands into an empire. Deep in the seemingly empty Sahara a secret drama is being played that stirs the passions of men. The true life of the desert is not made up of the marches of tribes in search of pasture, but of the game that goes endlessly on. What a difference in substance between the sands of submission and the sands of unruliness! The dunes, the salines, change their nature according as the code changes by which they are governed.

And is not all the world like this? Gazing at this transfigured desert I remember the games of my childhood—the dark and golden park we peopled with gods; the limitless kingdom we made of this square mile never thoroughly explored, never thoroughly charted. We created a secret civilization where footfalls had a meaning and things a savor known in no other world.

And when we grow to be men and live under other laws, what remains of that park filled with the shadows of childhood, magical, freezing, burning? What do we learn when we return to it and stroll with a sort of despair along the outside of its little wall of gray stone, marveling that within a space so small we should have founded a kingdom that had seemed to us infinite—what do we learn except that in this infinity we shall never again set foot, and that it is into the game and not the park that we have lost the power to enter?

· 8 ·

Prisoner of the Sand

AFTER three years of life in the desert, I was transferred out. The fortunes of the air service sent
me wandering here and there until one day
I decided to attempt a long-distance flight from Paris
to Saïgon. When, on December 29, 1935, I took off, I
had no notion that the sands were preparing for me
their ultimate and culminating ordeal.

This is the story of the Paris-Saïgon flight.

I paid my final visit to the weather bureau, where I
found Monsieur Viaud stooped over his maps like a medi-

eval alchemist over an alembic. Lucas had come with me, and we stared together at the curving lines marking the new-sprung winds. With their tiny flying arrows, they put me in mind of curving tendrils studded with thorns. All the atmospheric depressions of the world were charted on this enormous map, ochre-colored, like the earth of Asia.

"Here is a storm that we'll not hear from before Monday," Monsieur Viaud pointed out.

Over Russia and the Scandinavian peninsula the swirling lines took the form of a coiled demon. Out in Iraq, in the neighborhood of Basra, an imp was whirling.

"That fellow worries me a little," said Monsieur Viaud.

"Sand-storm, is it?"

I was not being idly curious. Day would not yet be breaking when I reached Basra and I was fearful of flying at night in one of those desert storms that turn the sky into a yellow furnace and wipe out hills, towns, and river-banks, drowning earth and sky in one great conflagration. It would be bad enough to fly in daylight through a chaos in which the very elements themselves were indistinguishable.

"Sand-storm? No, not exactly."

"So much the better," I said to myself, and I looked round the room. I liked this laboratory atmosphere. Viaud, I felt, was a man escaped from the world. When he came in here and hung up his hat and coat on the

peg, he hung up with them all the confusion in which
the rest of mankind lived. Family cares, thoughts of in-
come, concerns of the heart—all that vanished on the
threshold of this room as at the door of a hermit's cell,
or an astronomer's tower, or a radio operator's shack.
Here was one of those men who are able to lock themselves up in the secrecy of their retreat and hold discourse with the universe.

Gently, for he was reflecting, Monsieur Viaud rubbed
the palms of his hands together.

"No, not a sand-storm. See here."

His finger traveled over the map and pointed out why.

At four in the morning Lucas shook me into consciousness.

"Wake up!"

And before I could so much as rub my eyes he was
saying, "Look here, at this report. Look at the moon.
You won't see much of her tonight. She's new, not very
bright, and she'll set at ten o'clock. And here's something else for you: sunrise in Greenwich Meridian Time
and in local time as well. And here: here are your maps,
with your course all marked out. And here—"

"—is your bag packed for Saïgon," my wife broke in.

A razor and a change of shirt. He who would travel
happily must travel light.

We got into a car and motored out to Le Bourget
while Fate spying in ambush put the finishing touches

to her plans. Those favorable winds that were to wheel in the heavens, that moon that was to sink at ten o'clock, were so many strategic positions at which Fate was assembling her forces.

It was cold at the airport, and dark. The *Simoon* was wheeled out of her hangar. I walked round my ship, stroking her wings with the back of my hand in a caress that I believe was love. Eight thousand miles I had flown in her, and her engines had not skipped a beat; not a bolt in her had loosened. This was the marvel that was to save our lives the next night by refusing to be ground to powder on meeting the upsurging earth.

Friends had turned up. Every long flight starts in the same atmosphere, and nobody who has experienced it once would ever have it otherwise: the wind, the drizzle at daybreak, the engines purring quietly as they are warmed up; this instrument of conquest gleaming in her fresh coat of "dope"—all of it goes straight to the heart.

Already one has a foretaste of the treasures about to be garnered on the way—the green and brown and yellow lands promised by the maps; the rosary of resounding names that make up the pilot's beads; the hours to be picked up one by one on the eastward flight into the sun.

There is a particular flavor about the tiny cabin in which, still only half awake, you stow away your thermos flasks and odd parts and over-night bag; in the fuel tanks heavy with power; and best of all, forward, in the magical instruments set like jewels in their panel and glimmering like a constellation in the dark of night. The mineral glow of the artificial horizon, these stethoscopes designed to take the heart-beat of the heavens, are things a pilot loves. The cabin of a plane is a world unto itself, and to the pilot it is home.

I took off, and though the load of fuel was heavy, I got easily away. I avoided Paris with a jerk and up the Seine, at Melun, I found myself flying very low between showers of rain. I was heading for the valley of the Loire. Nevers lay below me, and then Lyon. Over the Rhône I was shaken up a bit. Mt. Ventoux was capped in snow. There lies Marignane and here comes Marseille.

The towns slipped past as in a dream. I was going so far—or thought I was going so far—that these wretched little distances were covered before I was aware of it. The minutes were flying. So much the better. There are times when, after a quarter-hour of flight, you look at your watch and find that five minutes have gone by; other days when the hands turn a quarter of an hour in the wink of an eye. This was a day when time was flying. A good omen. I started out to sea.

Very odd, that little stream of vapor rising from the fuel gauge on my port wing! It might almost be a plume of smoke.

"Prévot!"

My mechanic leaned towards me.

"Look! Isn't that gas? Seems to me it's leaking pretty fast."

He had a look and shook his head.

"Better check our consumption," I said.

I wasn't turning back yet. My course was still set for Tunis. I looked round and could see Prévot at the gauge on the second fuel tank aft. He came forward and said:

"You've used up about fifty gallons."

Nearly twenty had leaked away in the wind! That was serious. I put back to Marignane where I drank a cup of coffee while the time lost hurt like an open wound. Flyers in the Air France service wanted to know whether I was bound for Saïgon or Madagascar and wished me luck. The tank was patched up and re-filled, and I took off once more with a full load, again without mishap despite a bit of rough going over the soggy field.

As soon as I reached the sea I ran into low-hanging clouds that forced me down to sixty feet. The driving rain spattered against the windshield and the sea was churning and foaming. I strained to see ahead and keep from hooking the mast of some ship, while Prévot lit cigarettes for me.

"Coffee!"

He vanished into the stern of the cockpit and came back with the thermos flask. I drank. From time to time I flicked the throttle to keep the engines at exactly 2100 revolutions and ran my eye over the dials like a captain inspecting his troops. My company stood trim and erect: every needle was where it should be.

I glanced down at the sea and saw it bubbling under the steaming rain like a boiling cauldron. In a hydroplane this bumpy sea would have bothered me; but in this ship of mine, which could not possibly be set down here, I felt differently. It was silly, of course, but the thought gave me a sense of security. The sea was part of a world that I had nothing to do with. Engine trouble here was out of the question: there was not the least danger of such a thing. Why, I was not rigged for the sea!

After an hour and a half of this, the rain died down, and though the clouds still hung low a genial sun began to break through. I was immensely cheered by this promise of good weather. Overhead I could feel a thin layer of cotton-wool and I swerved aside to avoid a downpour. I was past the point where I had to cut through the heart of squalls. Was not that the first rift in the cloud-bank, there ahead of me?

I sensed it before I saw it, for straight ahead on the sea lay a long meadow-colored swath, a sort of oasis of deep and luminous green reminding me of those barley fields in southern Morocco that would make me catch my breath each time I sighted them on coming up from Senegal across two thousand miles of sand. Here as at such times in Morocco I felt we had reached a place a man could live in, and it bucked me up. I flung a glance backward at Prévot and called out:

"We're over the worst of it. This is fine."

"Yes," he said, "fine."

This meant that I would not need to do any stunt flying when Sardinia hove unexpectedly into view. The island would not loom up suddenly like a mass of wreckage a hundred feet ahead of me: I should be able to see it rising on the horizon in the distant play of a thousand sparkling points of light.

I moved into this region bathed by the sun. No doubt about it, I was loafing along. Loafing at the rate of one hundred and seventy miles an hour, but loafing nevertheless. I smoked a few leisurely cigarettes. I lingered over my coffee. I kept a cautious fatherly eye on my brood of instruments. These clouds, this sun, this play of light, lent to my flight the relaxation of a Sunday afternoon stroll. The sea was as variegated as a country landscape broken into fields of green and violet and blue. Off in the distance, just where a squall was blowing, I could see the fermenting spray. Once again I recognized that the sea was of all things in the world the least monotonous, was formed of an ever-changing substance. A gust of wind mantles it with light or strips it bare. I turned back to Prévot.

"Look!" I said.

There in the distance lay the shores of Sardinia that we were about to skirt to the southward.

Prévot came forward and sat down beside me. He squinted with wrinkled forehead at the mountains struggling out of their shroud of mist. The clouds had been blown away and the island was coming into view in great slabs of field and woodland. I climbed to forty-five hundred feet and drifted along the coast of this island dotted with villages. After the flower-strewn but uninhabitable sea, this was a place where I could take things easily. For a little time I clung to our great-hearted mother earth. Then, Sardinia behind me, I headed for Tunis.

I picked up the African continent at Bizerta and there I began to drop earthward. I was at home. Here was a place where I could dispense with altitude which, as every pilot knows, is our particular store of wealth. Not that we squander it when it is no longer needed: we swap it for another kind of treasure. When a flyer is within a quarter of an hour of port, he sets his controls for the down swing, throttling his motor a little—just enough to keep it from racing while the needle on his speedometer swings round from one hundred and seventy to two hundred miles an hour.

At that rate of speed the impalpable eddies of evening air drum softly on the wings and the plane seems to be drilling its way into a quivering crystal so delicate that the wake of a passing swallow would jar it to bits. I was already skirting the undulations of the hills and had given away almost the whole of my few hundred feet of altitude when I reached the airdrome, and there, shaving the roofs of the hangars, I set down my ship on the ground.

While the tanks were being re-filled I signed some papers and shook hands with a few friends. And just as I was coming out of the administration building I heard a horrible grunt, one of those muffled impacts that tell their fatal story in a single sound; one of those echoless thuds complete in themselves, without appeal, in which fatality delivers its message. Instantly there came into my mind the memory of an identical sound—an explosion in a garage. Two men had died of that hoarse bark.

I looked now across to the road that ran alongside the airdrome: there in a puff of dust two high-powered cars had crashed head-on and stood frozen into motionlessness as if imprisoned in ice. Men were running towards the cars while others ran from them to the field office.

"Get a doctor. . . . Skull crushed. . . ."

My heart sank. In the peace of the evening light Fate had taken a trick. A beauty, a mind, a life—something had been destroyed. It was as sudden as a raid in the desert. Marauding tribesmen creep up on silent feet in the night. The camp resounds briefly with the clashing tumult of a razzia. A moment later everything has sunk back into the golden silence. The same peace, the same stillness, followed this crash.

Near by, someone spoke of a fractured skull. I had no mind to be told about that crushed and bloody cranium. Turning my back to the road, I went across to my ship, in my heart a foreboding of danger. I was to recognize that sound when I heard it again very soon. When the *Simoon* scraped the black plateau at a speed of one hundred and seventy miles an hour I should recognize that hoarse grunt, that same snarl of destiny keeping its appointment with us.

Off to Benghazi! We still have two hours of daylight. Before we crossed into Tripolitana I took off my glare glasses. The sands were golden under the slanting rays of the sun. How empty of life is this planet of ours! Once again it struck me that its rivers, its woods, its human habitations were the product of chance, of fortuitous conjunctions of circumstance. What a deal of the earth's surface is given over to rock and sand!

But all this was not my affair. My world was the world of flight. Already I could feel the oncoming night within which I should be enclosed as in the precincts of a temple—enclosed in the temple of night for the accomplishment of secret rites and absorption in inviolable contemplation.

Already this profane world was beginning to fade out: soon it would vanish altogether. This landscape was still laved in golden sunlight, but already something was evaporating out of it. I know nothing, nothing in the world, equal to the wonder of nightfall in the air.

Those who have been enthralled by the witchery of flying will know what I mean—and I do not speak of the men who, among other sports, enjoy taking a turn in a plane. I speak of those who fly professionally and have sacrificed much to their craft. Mermoz said once, "It's worth it, it's worth the final smash-up."

No question about it; but the reason is hard to formulate. A novice taking orders could appreciate this ascension towards the essence of things, since his profession too is one of renunciation: he renounces the world; he renounces riches; he renounces the love of woman. And by renunciation he discovers his hidden god.

I, too, in this flight, am renouncing things. I am giving up the broad golden surfaces that would befriend me if my engines were to fail. I am giving up the landmarks by which I might be taking my bearings. I am giving up the profiles of mountains against the sky that would warn me of pitfalls. I am plunging into the night. I am navigating. I have on my side only the stars.

The diurnal death of the world is a slow death. It is only little by little that the divine beacon of daylight recedes from me. Earth and sky begin to merge into each other. The earth rises and seems to spread like a mist. The first stars tremble as if shimmering in green water. Hours must pass before their glimmer hardens into the frozen glitter of diamonds. I shall have a long wait before I witness the soundless frolic of the shooting stars. In the profound darkness of certain nights I have seen the sky streaked with so many trailing sparks that it seemed to me a great gale must be blowing through the outer heavens.

Prévot was testing the lamps in their sockets and the emergency torches. Round the bulbs he was wrapping red paper.

"Another layer."

He added another wrapping of paper and touched a switch. The dim light within the plane was still too bright. As in a photographer's dark-room, it veiled the pale picture of the external world. It hid that glowing phosphorescence which sometimes, at night, clings to the surface of things. Now night has fallen, but it is not yet true night. A crescent moon persists.

Prévot dove aft and came back with a sandwich. I nibbled a bunch of grapes. I was not hungry. I was neither hungry nor thirsty. I felt no weariness. It seemed to me that I could go on like this at the controls for ten years. I was happy.

The moon had set. It was pitch dark when we came in sight of Benghazi. The town lay at the bottom of an obscurity so dense that it was without a halo. I saw the place only when I was over it. As I was hunting for the airdrome the red obstruction lights were switched on. They cut out a black rectangle in the earth.

I banked, and at that moment the rays of a floodlight rose into the sky like a jet from a fire-hose. It pivoted and traced a golden lane over the landing-field. I circled again to get a clear view of what might be in my way. The port was equipped with everything to make a night-landing easy. I throttled down my engine and dropped like a diver into black water.

It was eleven o'clock local time when I landed and taxied across to the beacon. The most helpful ground crew in the world wove in and out of the blinding ray of a searchlight, alternately visible and invisible. They took my papers and began promptly to fill my tanks. Twenty minutes of my time was all they asked for, and I was touched by their great readiness to help. As I was taking off, one of them said:

"Better circle round and fly over us; otherwise we shan't be sure you got off all right."

I rolled down the golden lane towards an unimpeded opening. My *Simoon* lifted her overload clear of the ground well before I reached the end of the runway. The searchlight following me made it hard for me to wheel. Soon it let me go: the men on the ground had guessed that it was dazzling me. I turned right about and banked vertically, and at that moment the searchlight caught me between the eyes again; but scarcely had it touched me when it fled and sent elsewhere its long golden flute. I knew that the ground crew were being most thoughtful and I was grateful. And now I was off to the desert.

All along the line, at Paris, at Tunis, and at Bengñazi, I had been told that I should have a following wind of up to twenty-five miles an hour. I was counting on a speed of 190 m.p.h. as I set my course on the middle of the stretch between Alexandria and Cairo. On this course I should avoid the danger zones along the coast, and despite any drifting I might do without knowing it, I should pick up either to port or to starboard the lights of one of those two cities. Failing them I should certainly not miss the lights of the Nile valley. With a steady wind I should reach the Nile in three hours and twenty minutes; if the wind fell, three hours and three-quarters. Calculating thus I began to eat up the six hundred and fifty miles of desert ahead of me.

There was no moon. The world was a bubble of pitch that had dilated until it reached the very stars in the heavens. I should not see a single gleam of light, should not profit by the faintest landmark. Carrying no wireless, I should receive no message from the earth until I reached the Nile. It was useless to try to look at anything other than the compass and the artificial horizon. I might blot the world out of my mind and concentrate my attention upon the slow pulsation of the narrow thread of radium paint that ran along the dark background of the dials.

Whenever Prévot stirred I brought the plane

smoothly back to plumb. I went up to six thousand feet where I had been told the winds would be favorable. At long intervals I switched on a lamp to glance at the engine dials, not all of which were phosphorescent; but most of the time I wrapped myself closely round in darkness among my miniature constellations which gave off the same mineral glow as the stars, the same mysterious and unwearied light, and spoke the same language.

Like the astronomers, I too was reading in the book of celestial mechanics. I too seemed to myself studious and uncorrupted. Everything in the world that might have lured me from my studies had gone out. The external world had ceased to exist.

There was Prévot, who, after a vain resistance, had fallen asleep and left me to the greater enjoyment of my solitude. There was the gentle purr of my beautiful little motor, and before me, on the instrument panel, there were all those tranquil stars. I was most decidedly not sleepy. If this state of quiet well-being persisted until tomorrow night, I intended to push on without a stop to Saïgon.

Now the flight was beginning to seem to me short. Benghazi, the only troublesome night-landing on the route, had banked its fires and settled down behind the horizon in that dark shuttering in which cities take their slumber.

Meanwhile I was turning things over in my mind. We were without the moon's help and we had no wireless. No slightest tenuous tie was to bind us to earth until the Nile showed its thread of light directly ahead of us. We were truly alone in the universe—a thought that caused me not the least worry. If my motor were to cough, that sound would startle me more than if my heart should skip a beat.

Into my mind came the image of Sabathier, the white-haired engineer with the clear eye. I was thinking that, from one point of view, it would be hard to draw a distinction in the matter of human values between a profession like his and that of the painter, the composer, or the poet. I could see in the mind's eye those watchmaker's hands of his that had brought into being this clockwork I was piloting. Men who have given their lives to labors of love go straight to my heart.

"Couldn't I change this?" I had asked him.

"I shouldn't advise it," he had answered.

I was remembering our last conversation. He had thought it inadvisable, and of course that had settled it. A physician, that's it! Exactly the way one puts oneself into the hands of one's doctor—when he has that look in his eye. It was by his motor that we hung suspended in air and were able to go on living with the ticking of time in this penetrable pitch. We were crossing the great dark valley of a fairy-tale, the Valley of Ordeal. Like the prince in the tale, we must meet the test without succor. Failure here would not be forgiven. We were in the lap of the inexorable gods.

A ray of light was filtering through a joint in the lamp shaft. I woke up Prévot and told him to put it out. Prévot stirred in the darkness like a bear, snorted, and came forward. He fumbled for a bit with handkerchiefs and black paper, and the ray of light vanished. That light had bothered me because it was not of my world. It swore at the pale and distant gleam of the phosphorescence and was like a night-club spotlight compared to the gleam of a star. Besides, it had dazzled me and had out-shone all else that gleamed.

We had been flying for three hours. A brightness that seemed to me a glare spurted on the starboard side. I stared. A streamer of light which I had hitherto not noticed was fluttering from a lamp at the tip of the wing. It was an intermittent glow, now brilliant, now dim. It told me that I had flown into a cloud, and it was on the cloud that the lamp was reflected.

I was nearing the landmarks upon which I had counted; a clear sky would have helped a lot. The wing shone bright under the halo. The light steadied itself, became fixed, and then began to radiate in the form of a bouquet of pink blossoms. Great eddies of air were swinging me to and fro. I was navigating somewhere in the belly of a cumulus whose thickness I could not guess. I rose to seventy-five hundred feet and was still in it. Down again to three thousand, and the bouquet of flowers was still with me, motionless and growing brighter.

Well, there it was and there was nothing to do about it. I would think of something else, and wait to get clear of it. Just the same, I did not like this sinister glitter of a one-eyed grog-shop.

"Let me think," I said to myself. "I am bouncing round a bit, but there's nothing abnormal about that. I've been bumped all the way, despite a clear sky and plenty of ceiling. The wind has not died down, and I must be doing better than the 190 m.p.h. I counted on." This was about as far as I could get. Oh, well, when I got through the cloud-bank I would try to take my bearings.

Out of it we flew. The bouquet suddenly vanished, letting me know I was in the clear again. I stared ahead and saw, if one can speak of "seeing" space, a narrow valley of sky and the wall of the next cumulus. Already the bouquet was coming to life again. I was free of that viscous mess from time to time but only for a few seconds each time. After three and a half hours of flying it began to get on my nerves. If I had made the time I imagined, we were certainly approaching the Nile. With a little luck I might be able to spot the river through the rifts, but they were getting rare. I dared not come down, for if I was actually slower than I thought, I was still over high-lying country.

Thus far I was entirely without anxiety; my only fear was that I might presently be wasting time. I decided that I would take things easy until I had flown four and a quarter hours: after that, even in a dead calm (which was highly unlikely) I should have crossed the Nile. When I reached the fringes of the cloud-bank the bouquet winked on and off more and more swiftly and then suddenly went out. Decidedly, I did not like these dot-and-dash messages from the demons of the night.

A green star appeared ahead of me, flashing like a lighthouse. Was it a lighthouse? or really a star? I took no pleasure from this supernatural gleam, this star the Magi might have seen, this dangerous decoy.

Prévot, meanwhile, had waked up and turned his electric torch on the engine dials. I waved him off, him and his torch. We had just sailed into the clear between two clouds and I was busy staring below. Prévot went back to sleep. The gap in the clouds was no help: there was nothing below.

Four hours and five minutes in the air. Prévot awoke and sat down beside me.

"I'll bet we're near Cairo," he said.

"We must be."

"What's that? A star? or is it a lighthouse?"

I had throttled the engine down a little. This, probably, was what had awakened Prévot. He is sensitive to all the variations of sound in flight.

I began a slow descent, intending to slip under the mass of clouds. Meanwhile I had had a look at my map. One thing was sure—the land below me lay at sea level, and there was no risk of conking against a hill. Down

I went, flying due north so that the lights of the cities would strike square into my windows. I must have over-flown them, and should therefore see them on my left.

Now I was flying below the cumulus. But alongside was another cloud hanging lower down on the left. I swerved so as not to be caught in its net, and headed north-northeast. This second cloud-bank certainly went down a long way, for it blocked my view of the horizon. I dared not give up any more altitude. My altimeter registered 1200 feet, but I had no notion of the atmospheric pressure here. Prévot leaned towards me and I shouted to him, "I'm going out to sea. I'd rather come down on it than risk a crash here."

As a matter of fact, there was nothing to prove that we had not drifted over the sea already. Below that cloud-bank visibility was exactly nil. I hugged my window, trying to read below me, to discover flares, signs of life. I was a man raking dead ashes, trying in vain to retrieve the flame of life in a hearth.

"A lighthouse!"

Both of us spied it at the same moment, that wink-ing decoy! What madness! Where was that phantom light, that invention of the night? For at the very second when Prévot and I leaned forward to pick it out of the air where it had glittered nine hundred feet below our wings, suddenly, at that very instant . . .

"Oh!"

I am quite sure that this was all I said. I am quite sure

that all I felt was a terrific crash that rocked our world to its foundations. We had crashed against the earth at a hundred and seventy miles an hour. I am quite sure that in the split second that followed, all I expected was the great flash of ruddy light of the explosion in which Prévot and I were to be blown up together. Neither he nor I had felt the least emotion of any kind. All I could observe in myself was an extraordinary tense feeling of expectancy, the expectancy of that resplendent star in which we were to vanish within the second.

But there was no ruddy star. Instead there was a sort of earthquake that splintered our cabin, ripped away the windows, blew sheets of metal hurtling through space a hundred yards away, and filled our very entrails with its roar. The ship quivered like a knife-blade thrown from a distance into a block of oak, and its anger mashed us as if we were so much pulp.

One second, two seconds passed, and the plane still quivered while I waited with a grotesque impatience for the forces within it to burst it like a bomb. But the subterranean quakings went on without a climax of eruption while I marveled uncomprehendingly at its invisible travail. I was baffled by the quaking, the anger, the interminable postponement. Five seconds passed; six seconds. And suddenly we were seized by a spinning motion, a shock that jerked our cigarettes out of the window, pulverized the starboard wing—and then nothing, nothing but a frozen immobility. I shouted to Prévot:

"Jump!"

And in that instant he cried out:

"Fire!"

We dove together through the wrecked window and found ourselves standing side by side, sixty feet from the plane. I said:

"Are you hurt?"

He answered:

"Not a bit."

But he was rubbing his knee.

"Better run your hands over yourself," I said; "move about a bit. Sure no bones are broken?"

He answered:

"I'm all right. It's that emergency pump."

Emergency pump! I was sure he was going to keel over any minute and split open from head to navel there before my eyes. But he kept repeating with a glassy stare:

"That pump, that emergency pump."

He's out of his head, I thought. He'll start dancing in a minute.

Finally he stopped staring at the plane—which had not gone up in flames—and stared at me instead. And he said again:

"I'm all right. It's that emergency pump. It got me in the knee."

Why we were not blown up, I do not know. I switched on my electric torch and went back over the furrow in the ground traced by the plane. Two hundred and fifty yards from where we stopped the ship had begun to shed the twisted iron and sheet-metal that spattered the sand the length of her traces. We were to see, when day came, that we had run almost tangentially into a gentle slope at the top of a barren plateau. At the point of impact there was a hole in the sand that looked as if it had been made by a plough. Maintaining an even keel, the plane had run its course with the fury and the tail-lashings of a reptile gliding on its belly at the rate of a hundred and seventy miles an hour. We owed our lives to the fact that this desert was surfaced with round black pebbles which had rolled over and over like ball-bearings beneath us. They must have rained upward to the heavens as we shot through them.

Prévot disconnected the batteries for fear of fire by short-circuit. I leaned against the motor and turned the situation over in my mind. I had been flying high for four hours and a quarter, possibly with a thirty-mile following wind. I had been jolted a good deal. If the wind had changed since the weather people forecast it, I was unable to say into what quarter it had veered. All I could make out was that we had crashed in an empty square two hundred and fifty miles on each side.

Prévot came up and sat down beside me.

"I can't believe that we're alive," he said.

I said nothing. Even that thought could not cheer me. A germ of an idea was at work in my mind and was already bothering me. Telling Prévot to switch on his torch as a landmark, I walked straight out, scrutinizing the ground in the light of my own torch as I went.

I went forward slowly, swung round in a wide arc, and changed direction a number of times. I kept my eyes fixed on the ground like a man hunting a lost ring.

Only a little while before I had been straining just as hard to see a gleam of light from the air. Through the darkness I went, bowed over the traveling disk of white light. "Just as I thought," I said to myself, and I went slowly back to the plane. I sat down beside the cabin and ruminated. I had been looking for a reason to hope and had failed to find it. I had been looking for a sign of life, and no sign of life had appeared.

"Prévot, I couldn't find a single blade of grass."

Prévot said nothing, and I was not sure he had understood. Well, we could talk about it again when the curtain rose at dawn. Meanwhile I was dead tired and all I could think was, "Two hundred and fifty miles more or less in the desert."

Suddenly I jumped to my feet. "Water!" I said.

Gas tanks and oil tanks were smashed in. So was our supply of drinking-water. The sand had drunk everything. We found a pint of coffee in a battered thermos flask and half a pint of white wine in another. We filtered both, and poured them into one flask. There were some grapes, too, and a single orange. Meanwhile I was computing: "All this will last us five hours of tramping in the sun."

We crawled into the cabin and waited for dawn. I stretched out, and as I settled down to sleep I took stock of our situation. We didn't know where we were; we had less than a quart of liquid between us; if we were not too far off the Benghazi-Cairo lane we should be found in a week, and that would be too late. Yet it was the best we could hope for. If, on the other hand, we had drifted off our course, we shouldn't be found in six months. One thing was sure—we could not count on being picked up by a plane; the men who came out for us would have two thousand miles to cover.

"You know, it's a shame," Prévot said suddenly.

"What's a shame?"

"That we didn't crash properly and have it over with."

It seemed pretty early to be throwing in one's hand. Prévot and I pulled ourselves together. There was still a chance, slender as it was, that we might be saved miraculously by a plane. On the other hand, we couldn't stay here and perhaps miss a near-by oasis. We would walk all day and come back to the plane before dark. And before going off we would write our plan in huge letters in the sand.

With this I curled up and settled down to sleep. I was happy to go to sleep. My weariness wrapped me round like a multiple presence. I was not alone in the desert: my drowsiness was peopled with voices and memories and whispered confidences. I was not yet thirsty; I felt strong; and I surrendered myself to sleep as to an aimless journey. Reality lost ground before the advance of dreams.

Ah, but things were different when I awoke!

In times past I have loved the Sahara. I have spent nights alone in the path of marauding tribes and have waked up with untroubled mind in the golden emptiness of the desert where the wind like a sea had raised sand-waves upon its surface. Asleep under the wing of my plane I have looked forward with confidence to being rescued next day. But this was not the Sahara!

Prévot and I walked along the slopes of rolling mounds. The ground was sand covered over with a single layer of shining black pebbles. They gleamed like metal scales and all the domes about us shone like coats of mail. We had dropped down into a mineral world and were hemmed in by iron hills.

When we reached the top of the first crest we saw in the distance another just like it, black and gleaming. As we walked we scraped the ground with our boots, marking a trail over which to return to the plane. We went forward with the sun in our eyes. It was not logical to go due east like this, for everything—the weather reports, the duration of the flight—had made it plain that we had crossed the Nile. But I had started tentatively towards the west and had felt a vague foreboding I could not explain to myself. So I had put off the west till to-morrow. In the same way, provisionally, I had given up going north, though that led to the sea.

Three days later, when scourged by thirst into aban-doning the plane and walking straight on until we dropped in our tracks, it was still eastward that we tramped. More precisely, we walked east-northeast. And this too was in defiance of all reason and even of all hope. Yet after we had been rescued we discovered that if we had gone in any other direction we should have been lost.

Northward, we should never have had the endur-ance to reach the sea. And absurd as it may appear, it seems to me now, since I had no other motive, that I must have chosen the east simply because it was by go-ing eastward that Guillaumet had been saved in the Andes, after I had hunted for him everywhere. In a confused way the east had become for me the direction of life.

We walked on for five hours and then the landscape changed. A river of sand seemed to be running through a valley, and we followed this river-bed, taking long strides in order to cover as much ground as possible and get back to the plane before night fell, if our march was in vain. Suddenly I stopped.

"Prévot!"

"What's up?"

"Our tracks!"

How long was it since we had forgotten to leave a wake behind us? We had to find it or die.

We went back, bearing to the right. When we had gone back far enough we would make a right angle to the left and eventually intersect our tracks where we had still remembered to mark them.

This we did and were off again. The heat rose and with it came the mirages. But these were still the commonplace kind—sheets of water that materialized and then vanished as we neared them. We decided to cross the valley of sand and climb the highest dome in order to look round the horizon. This was after six hours of march in which, striding along, we must have covered twenty miles.

When we had struggled up to the top of the black hump we sat down and looked at each other. At our feet lay our valley of sand, opening into a desert of sand whose dazzling brightness seared our eyes. As far as the eye could see lay empty space. But in that space the play of light created mirages which, this time, were of a disturbing kind, fortresses and minarets, angular geometric hulks. I could see also a black mass that pretended to be vegetation, overhung by the last of those clouds that dissolve during the day only to return at night. This mass of vegetation was the shadow of a cumulus.

It was no good going on. The experiment was a failure. We would have to go back to our plane, to that red and white beacon which, perhaps, would be picked out by a flyer. I was not staking great hopes on a rescue party, but it did seem to me our last chance of salvation. In any case, we had to get back to our few drops of liquid, for our throats were parched. We were imprisoned in this iron circle, captives of the curt dictatorship of thirst.

And yet, how hard it was to turn back when there was a chance that we might be on the road to life! Beyond the mirages the horizon was perhaps rich in veritable treasures, in meadows and runnels of sweet water. I knew I was doing the right thing by returning to the plane, and yet as I swung round and started back I was filled with portents of disaster.

We were resting on the ground beside the plane. Nearly forty miles of wandering this day. The last drop of liquid had been drained. No sign of life had appeared to the east. No plane had soared overhead. How long should we be able to hold out? Already our thirst was terrible.

We had built up a great pyre out of bits of the splintered wing. Our gasoline was ready, and we had flung on the heap sheets of metal whose magnesium coating would burn with a hard white flame. We were waiting now for night to come down before we lighted our conflagration. But where were there men to see it?

Night fell and the flames rose. Prayerfully we watched our mute and radiant fanion mount resplendent into the night. As I looked I said to myself that this message was not only a cry for help, it was fraught also with a great deal of love. We were begging water, but we were also begging the communion of human society. Only man can create fire: let another flame light up the night; let man answer man!

I was haunted by a vision of my wife's eyes under the halo of her hat. Of her face I could see only the eyes, questioning me, looking at me yearningly. I am answering, answering with all my strength! What flame could leap higher than this that darts up into the night from my heart?

What I could do, I have done. What we could do, we have done. Nearly forty miles, almost without a drop to drink. Now there was no water left. Was it our fault that we could wait no longer? Suppose we had sat quietly by the plane, taking suck at the mouths of our water-bottles? But from the moment I breathed in the moist bottom of the tin cup, a clock had started up in me. From the second when I had sucked up the last drop, I had begun to slip downhill. Could I help it if time like a river was carrying me away? Prévot was weeping. I tapped him on the shoulder and said, to console him:

"If we're done for we're done for, and that's all there is to it."

He said:

"Do you think it's me I'm bawling about?"

I might have known it. It was evident enough. Nothing is unbearable. Tomorrow, and the day after, I should learn that nothing was really unbearable. I had never really believed in torture. Reading Poe as a kid, I had already said as much to myself. Once, jammed in the cabin of a plane, I thought I was going to drown; and I had not suffered much. Several times it had seemed to me that the final smash-up was coming, and I don't remember that I thought of it as a cosmic event. And I didn't believe this was going to be agonizing either. There will be time tomorrow to find out stranger things about it. Meanwhile, God knows that despite the bonfire I had decidedly given up hope that our cries would be heard by the world.

"Do you think it's me . . ." There you have what is truly unbearable! Every time I saw those yearning eyes it was as if a flame were searing me. They were like a scream for help, like the flares of a sinking ship. I felt that I should not sit idly by: I should jump up and run— anywhere! straight ahead of me!

What a strange reversal of rôles! But I have always thought it would be like this. Still, I needed Prévot beside me to be quite sure of it. Prévot was a level-headed fellow. He loved life. And yet Prévot no more than I was wringing his hands at the sight of death the way we are told men do. But there did exist something that he could not bear any more than I could. I was perfectly ready to fall asleep, whether for a night or for eternity. If I did fall asleep, I could not even know whether it was for the one or for the other. And the peace of sleep! But that cry that would be sent up at home, that great wail of desolation—that was what I could not bear. I could not stand idly by and look on at that disaster. Each second of silence drove the knife deeper into someone I loved. At the thought, a blind rage surged up in me. Why do these chains bind me and prevent me from rescuing those who are drowning? Why does our conflagration not carry our cry to the ends of the world? Hear me, you out here! Patience. We are coming to save you.

The magnesium had been licked off and the metal was glowing red. There was left only a heap of embers round which we crouched to warm ourselves. Our flaming call had spent itself. Had it set anything in the world in motion? I knew well enough that it hadn't. Here was a prayer that had of necessity gone unheard.

That was that.

I ought to get some sleep.

At daybreak I took a rag and mopped up a little dew on the wings. The mixture of water and paint and oil yielded a spoonful of nauseating liquid which we sipped because it would at least moisten our lips. After this banquet Prévot said:

"Thank God we've got a gun."

Instantly I became furious and turned on him with an aggressiveness which I regretted directly I felt it. There was nothing I should have loathed more at that moment than a gush of sentimentality. I am so made that I have to believe that everything is simple. Birth is simple. Growing up is simple. And dying of thirst is simple. I watched Prévot out of the corner of my eye, ready to wound his feelings, if that was necessary to shut him up.

But Prévot had spoken without emotion. He had been discussing a matter of hygiene, and might have said in the same tone, "We ought to wash our hands." That being so, we were agreed. Indeed already yesterday, my eye falling by chance on the leather holster, the same thought had crossed my mind, and with me too it had been a reasonable reflex, not an emotional one. Pathos resides in social man, not in the individual; what was pathetic was our powerlessness to reassure those for whom we were responsible, not what we might do with the gun.

There was still no sign that we were being sought; or rather they were doubtless hunting for us elsewhere, probably in Arabia. We were to hear no sound of plane until the day after we had abandoned our own. And if ships did pass overhead, what could that mean to us? What could they see in us except two black dots among the thousand shadowy dots in the desert? Absurd to think of being distinguishable from them. None of the reflections that might be attributed to me on the score of this torture would be true. I should not feel in the least tortured. The aerial rescue party would seem to me, each time I sighted one, to be moving through a universe that was not mine. When searchers have to cover two thousand miles of territory, it takes them a good two weeks to spot a plane in the desert from the sky.

They were probably looking for us all along the line from Tripoli to Persia. And still, with all this, I clung to the slim chance that they might pick us out. Was that not our only chance of being saved? I changed my tactics, determining to go reconnoitering by myself. Prévot would get another bonfire together and kindle it in the event that visitors showed up. But we were to have no callers that day.

So off I went without knowing whether or not I should have the stamina to come back. I remembered what I knew about this Libyan desert. When, in the Sahara, humidity is still at forty per cent of saturation, it is only eighteen here in Libya. Life here evaporates like a vapor. Bedouins, explorers, and colonial officers all tell us that a man may go nineteen hours without water. Thereafter his eyes fill with light, and that marks the beginning of the end. The progress made by thirst is swift and terrible. But this northeast wind, this abnor-

mal wind that had blown us out off our course and had
marooned us on this plateau, was now prolonging our
lives. What was the length of the reprieve it would
grant us before our eyes began to fill with light? I went
forward with the feeling of a man canoeing in mid-
ocean.

I will admit that at daybreak this landscape seemed to
me less infernal, and that I began my walk with my
hands in my pockets, like a tramp on a highroad. The
evening before we had set snares at the mouths of certain mysterious burrows in the ground, and the poacher
in me was on the alert. I went first to have a look at our
traps. They were empty.

Well, this meant that I should not be drinking blood
today; and indeed I hadn't expected to. But though I
was not disappointed, my curiosity was aroused. What
was there in the desert for these animals to live on?
These were certainly the holes of fennecs, a long-eared
carnivorous sand-fox the size of a rabbit. I spotted the
tracks made by one of them, and gave way to the impulse to follow them. They led to a narrow stream of
sand where each footprint was plainly outlined and
where I marveled at the pretty palm formed by the three
toes spread fanwise on the sand.

I could imagine my little friend trotting blithely along
at dawn and licking the dew off the rocks. Here the
tracks were wider apart: my fennec had broken into a
run. And now I see that a companion has joined him and

they have trotted on side by side. These signs of a morning stroll gave me a strange thrill. They were signs of
life, and I loved them for that. I almost forgot that I was
thirsty.

Finally I came to the pasture-ground of my foxes.
Here, every hundred yards or so, I saw sticking up out
of the sand a small dry shrub, its twigs heavy with little
golden snails. The fennec came here at dawn to do his
marketing. And here I was able to observe another of
nature's mysteries.

My fennec did not stop at all the shrubs. There were
some weighed down with snails which he disdained.
Obviously he avoided them with some wariness. Others
he stopped at but did not strip of all they bore. He must
have picked out two or three shells and then gone on to
another restaurant. What was he up to? Was he nurseryman to the snails, encouraging their reproduction by
refraining from exhausting the stock on a given shrub,
or a given twig? Or was he amusing himself by delaying
repletion, putting off satiety in order to enhance the
pleasure he took from his morning stroll?

The tracks led me back to the hole in which he lived.
Doubtless my fennec crouched below, listening to me
and startled by the crunching of my footsteps. I said to
him:

"Fox, my little fox, I'm done for; but somehow that
doesn't prevent me from taking an interest in your
mood."

And there I stayed a bit, ruminating and telling myself that a man was able to adapt himself to anything. The notion that he is to die in thirty years has probably never spoiled any man's fun. Thirty years . . . or thirty days: it's all a matter of perspective.

Only, you have to be able to put certain visions out of your mind.

I went on, finally, and the time came when, along with my weariness, something in me began to change. If those were not mirages, I was inventing them.

"Hi! Hi, there!"

I shouted and waved my arms, but the man I had seen waving at me turned out to be a black rock. Everything in the desert had grown animate. I stooped to waken a sleeping Bedouin and he turned into the trunk of a black tree. A tree-trunk? Here in the desert? I was amazed and bent over to lift a broken bough. It was solid marble.

Straightening up I looked round and saw more black marble. An antediluvian forest littered the ground with its broken tree-tops. How many thousand years ago, under what hurricane of the time of Genesis, had this cathedral of wood crumbled in this spot? Countless centuries had rolled these fragments of giant pillars at my feet, polished them like steel, petrified and vitrified them and indued them with the color of jet.

I could distinguish the knots in their branches, the

twistings of their once living boughs, could count the rings of life in them. This forest had rustled with birds and been filled with music that now was struck by doom and frozen into salt. And all this was hostile to me. Blacker than the chain-mail of the hummocks, these solemn derelicts rejected me. What had I, a living man, to do with this incorruptible stone? Perishable as I was, I whose body was to crumble into dust, what place had I in this eternity?

Since yesterday I had walked nearly fifty miles. This dizziness that I felt came doubtless from my thirst. Or from the sun. It glittered on these hulks until they shone as if smeared with oil. It blazed down on this universal carapace. Sand and fox had no life here. This world was a gigantic anvil upon which the sun beat down. I strode across this anvil and at my temples I could feel the hammer-strokes of the sun.

"Hi! Hi, there!" I called out.

"There is nothing there," I told myself. "Take it easy. You are delirious."

I had to talk to myself aloud, had to bring myself to reason. It was hard for me to reject what I was seeing, hard not to run towards that caravan plodding on the horizon. There! Do you see it?

"Fool! You know very well that you are inventing it."

"You mean that nothing in the world is real?"

Nothing in the world is real if that cross which I see ten miles off on the top of a hill is not real. Or is it a lighthouse? No, the sea does not lie in that direction. Then it must be a cross.

I had spent the night studying my map—but uselessly, since I did not know my position. Still, I had scrutinized all the signs that marked the marvelous presence of man. And somewhere on the map I had seen a little circle surmounted by just such a cross. I had glanced down at the legend to get an explanation of the symbol and had read: "Religious institution."

Close to the cross there had been a black dot. Again I had run my finger down the legend and had read: "Permanent well." My heart had jumped and I had repeated the legend aloud: "Permanent well, permanent well." What were all of Ali Baba's treasures compared with a permanent well? A little farther on were two white circles. "Temporary wells," the legend said. Not quite so exciting. And round about them was nothing . . . unless it was the blankness of despair.

But this must be my "religious institution"! The monks must certainly have planted a great cross on the hill expressly for men in our plight! All I had to do was to walk across to them. I should be taken in by those Dominicans. . . .

"But there are only Coptic monasteries in Libya!" I told myself.

. . . by those learned Dominicans. They have a great cool kitchen with red tiles, and out in the courtyard a marvelous rusted pump. Beneath the rusted pump; beneath the rusted pump . . . you've guessed it! . . . beneath the rusted pump is dug the permanent well! Ah, what rejoicing when I ring at their gate, when I get my hands on the rope of the great bell.

"Madman! You are describing a house in Provence; and what's more, the house has no bell!"

. . . on the rope of the great bell. The porter will raise his arms to Heaven and cry out, "You are the messenger of the Lord!" and he will call aloud to all the monks. They will pour out of the monastery. They will welcome me with a great feast, as if I were the Prodigal Son. They will lead me to the kitchen and will say to me, "One moment, my son, one moment. We'll just be off to the permanent well." And I shall be trembling with happiness.

No, no! I will *not* weep just because there happens to be no cross on the hill.

The treasures of the west turned out to be mere illusion. I have veered due north. At least the north is filled with the sound of the sea.

Over the hilltop. Look there, at the horizon! The most beautiful city in the world!

"You know perfectly well that is a mirage."

Of course I know it is a mirage! Am I the sort of man who can be fooled? But what if I *want* to go after that mirage? Suppose I enjoy indulging my hope? Suppose it suits me to love that crenelated town all beflagged with sunlight? What if I choose to walk straight ahead on light feet—for you must know that I have dropped my weariness behind me, I am happy now. . . . Prévot and his gun! Don't make me laugh! I prefer my drunkenness. I am drunk. I am dying of thirst.

It took the twilight to sober me. Suddenly I stopped, appalled to think how far I was from our base. In the twilight the mirage was dying. The horizon had stripped itself of its pomp, its palaces, its priestly vestments. It was the old desert horizon again.

"A fine day's work you've done! Night will overtake you. You won't be able to go on before daybreak, and by that time your tracks will have been blown away and you'll be properly nowhere."

In that case I may as well walk straight on. Why turn back? Why should I bring my ship round when I may find the sea straight ahead of me?

"When did you catch a glimpse of the sea? What makes you think you could walk that far? Meanwhile there's Prévot watching for you beside the *Simoon*. He may have been picked up by a caravan, for all you know."

Very good. I'll go back. But first I want to call out for help.

"Hi! Hi!"

By God! You can't tell me this planet is not inhabited. Where are its men?

"Hi! Hi!"

I was hoarse. My voice was gone. I knew it was ridiculous to croak like this, but—one more try:

"Hi! Hi!"

And I turned back.

I had been walking two hours when I saw the flames of the bonfire that Prévot, frightened by my long absence, had sent up. They mattered very little to me now.

Another hour of trudging. Five hundred yards away. A hundred yards. Fifty yards.

"Good Lord!"

Amazement stopped me in my tracks. Joy surged up and filled my heart with its violence. In the firelight stood Prévot, talking to two Arabs who were leaning against the motor. He had not noticed me, for he was too full of his own joy. If only I had sat still and waited with him! I should have been saved already. Exultantly I called out:

"Hi! Hi!"

The two Bedouins gave a start and stared at me. Prévot left them standing and came forward to meet me. I opened my arms to him. He caught me by the elbow. Did he think I was keeling over? I said:

"At last, eh?"

"What do you mean?"

"The Arabs!"

"What Arabs?"

"Those Arabs there, with you."

Prévot looked at me queerly, and when he spoke I felt as if he was very reluctantly confiding a great secret to me:

"There are no Arabs here."

This time I know I am going to cry.

A man can go nineteen hours without water, and what have we drunk since last night? A few drops of dew at dawn. But the northeast wind is still blowing, still slowing up the process of our evaporation. To it, also, we owe the continued accumulation of high clouds. If only they would drift straight overhead and break into rain! But it never rains in the desert.

"Look here, Prévot. Let's rip up one of the parachutes and spread the sections out on the ground, weighed down with stones. If the wind stays in the same quarter till morning, they'll catch the dew and we can wring them out into one of the tanks."

We spread six triangular sections of parachute under the stars, and Prévot unhooked a fuel tank. This was as much as we could do for ourselves till dawn. But, miracle of miracles! Prévot had come upon an orange while working over the tank. We shared it, and though it was little enough to men who could have used a few gallons of sweet water, still I was overcome with relief.

Stretched out beside the fire I looked at the glowing fruit and said to myself that men did not know what an orange was. "Here we are, condemned to death," I said to myself, "and still the certainty of dying cannot compare with the pleasure I am feeling. The joy I take from this half of an orange which I am holding in my hand is one of the greatest joys I have ever known."

I lay flat on my back, sucking my orange and counting the shooting stars. Here I was, for one minute infinitely happy. "Nobody can know anything of the world in which the individual moves and has his being," I reflected. "There is no guessing it. Only the man locked up in it can know what it is."

For the first time I understood the cigarette and glass of rum that are handed to the criminal about to be executed. I used to think that for a man to accept these wretched gifts at the foot of the gallows was beneath human dignity. Now I was learning that he took pleasure from them. People thought him courageous when he smiled as he smoked or drank. I knew now that he smiled because the taste gave him pleasure. People could not see that his perspective had changed, and that for him the last hour of his life was a life in itself.

We collected an enormous quantity of water—perhaps as much as two quarts. Never again would we be thirsty! We were saved; we had a liquid to drink!

I dipped my tin cup into the tank and brought up a beautifully yellow-green liquid the first mouthful of which nauseated me so that despite my thirst I had to catch my breath before swallowing it. I would have swallowed mud, I swear; but this taste of poisonous metal cut keener than thirst.

I glanced at Prévot and saw him going round and round with his eyes fixed to the ground as if looking for something. Suddenly he leaned forward and began to vomit without interrupting his spinning. Half a minute later it was my turn. I was seized by such convulsions that I went down on my knees and dug my fingers into the sand while I puked. Neither of us spoke, and for a quarter of an hour we remained thus shaken, bringing up nothing but a little bile.

After a time it passed and all I felt was a vague, distant nausea. But our last hope had fled. Whether our bad luck was due to a sizing on the parachute or to the magnesium lining of the tank, I never found out. Certain it was that we needed either another set of cloths or another receptacle.

Well, it was broad daylight and time we were on our way. This time we should strike out as fast as we could, leave this cursed plateau, and tramp till we dropped in our tracks. That was what Guillaumet had done in the Andes. I had been thinking of him all the day before and had determined to follow his example. I should do violence to the pilot's unwritten law, which is to stick by the ship; but I was sure no one would be along to look for us here.

Once again we discovered that it was not we who were shipwrecked, not we but those who were waiting for news of us, those who were alarmed by our silence, were already torn with grief by some atrocious and fantastic report. We could not but strive towards them. Guillaumet had done it, had scrambled towards his lost ones. To do so is a universal impulse.

"If I were alone in the world," Prévot said, "I'd lie down right here. Damned if I wouldn't."

East-northeast we tramped. If we had in fact crossed the Nile, each step was leading us deeper and deeper into the desert.

I don't remember anything about that day. I remember only my haste. I was hurrying desperately towards something—towards some finality. I remember also that I walked with my eyes to the ground, for the mirages were more than I could bear. From time to time we would correct our course by the compass, and now and again we would lie down to catch our breath. I remember having flung away my waterproof, which I had held on to as covering for the night. That is as much as I recall about the day. Of what happened when the chill of evening came, I remember more. But during the day I had simply turned to sand and was a being without mind.

When the sun set we decided to make camp. Oh, I knew as well as anybody that we should push on, that this one waterless night would finish us off. But we had brought along the bits of parachute, and if the poison was not in the sizing, we might get a sip of water next morning. Once again we spread our trap for the dew under the stars.

But the sky in the north was cloudless. The wind no longer had the same taste on the lip. It had moved into another quarter. Something was rustling against us, but this time it seemed to be the desert itself. The wild beast was stalking us, had us in its power. I could feel its breath in my face, could feel it lick my face and hands. Suppose I walked on: at the best I could do five or six miles more. Remember that in three days I had covered one hundred miles, practically without water.

And then, just as we stopped, Prévot said:

"I swear to you I see a lake!"

"You're crazy."

"Have you ever heard of a mirage after sunset?" he challenged.

I didn't seem able to answer him. I had long ago given up believing my own eyes. Perhaps it was not a mirage; but in that case it was a hallucination. How could Prévot go on believing? But he was stubborn about it.

"It's only twenty minutes off. I'll go have a look."

His mulishness got on my nerves.

"Go ahead!" I shouted. "Take your little constitutional. Nothing better for a man. But let me tell you, if your lake exists it is salt. And whether it's salt or not, it's a devil of a way off. And besides, there is no damned lake!"

Prévot was already on his way, his eyes glassy. I knew the strength of these irresistible obsessions. I was thinking: "There are somnambulists who walk straight into locomotives." And I knew that Prévot would not come back. He would be seized by the vertigo of empty space and would be unable to turn back. And then he would keel over. He somewhere, and I somewhere else. Not that it was important.

Thinking thus, it struck me that this mood of resignation was doing me no good. Once when I was half drowned I had let myself go like this. Lying now flat on my face on the stony ground, I took this occasion to write a letter for posthumous delivery. It gave me a chance, also, to take stock of myself again. I tried to bring up a little saliva: how long was it since I had spit? No saliva. If I kept my mouth closed, a kind of glue sealed my lips together. It dried on the outside of the lips and formed a hard crust. However, I found I was still able to swallow, and I bethought me that I was still not seeing a blinding light in my eyes. Once I was treated to that radiant spectacle I might know that the end was a couple of hours away.

Night fell. The moon had swollen since I last saw it. Prévot was still not back. I stretched out on my back and turned these few data over in my mind. A familiar impression came over me, and I tried to seize it. I was . . . I was . . . I was at sea. I was on a ship going to South America and was stretched out, exactly like this, on the boat deck. The tip of the mast was swaying to and fro, very slowly, among the stars. That mast was missing tonight, but again I was at sea, bound for a port I was to make without raising a finger. Slave-traders had flung me on this ship.

I thought of Prévot who was still not back. Not once had I heard him complain. That was a good thing. To hear him whine would have been unbearable. Prévot was a man.

What was that! Five hundred yards ahead of me I could see the light of his lamp. He had lost his way. I had no lamp with which to signal back. I stood up and shouted, but he could not hear me.

A second lamp, and then a third! God in Heaven! It was a search party and it was me they were hunting!

"Hi! Hi!" I shouted.

But they had not heard me. The three lamps were still signaling me.

"Tonight I am sane," I said to myself. "I am relaxed. I am not out of my head. Those are certainly three lamps and they are about five hundred yards off." I stared at them and shouted again, and again I gathered that they could not hear me.

Then, for the first and only time, I was really seized with panic. I could still run, I thought. "Wait! Wait!" I screamed. They seemed to be turning away from me, going off, hunting me elsewhere! And I stood tottering, tottering on the brink of life when there were arms out there ready to catch me! I shouted and screamed again and again.

They had heard me! An answering shout had come. I was strangling, suffocating, but I ran on, shouting as I ran, until I saw Prévot and keeled over.

When I could speak again I said: "Whew! When I saw all those lights . . ."

"What lights?"

God in Heaven, it was true! He was alone!

This time I was beyond despair. I was filled with a sort of dumb fury.

"What about your lake?" I rasped.

"As fast as I moved towards it, it moved back. I walked after it for about half an hour. Then it seemed still too far away, so I came back. But I am positive, now, that it is a lake."

"You're crazy. Absolutely crazy. Why did you do it? Tell me. Why?"

What had he done? Why had he done it? I was ready to weep with indignation, yet I scarcely knew why I was so indignant. Prévot mumbled his excuse:

"I felt I had to find some water. You . . . your lips were awfully pale."

Well! My anger died within me. I passed my hand over my forehead as if I were waking out of sleep. I was suddenly sad. I said:

"There was no mistake about it. I saw them as clearly

as I see you now. Three lights there were. I tell you, Prévot, I saw them!"

Prévot made no comment.

"Well," he said finally, "I guess we're in a bad way."

In this air devoid of moisture the soil is swift to give off its temperature. It was already very cold. I stood up and stamped about. But soon a violent fit of trembling came over me. My dehydrated blood was moving sluggishly and I was pierced by a freezing chill which was not merely the chill of night. My teeth were chattering and my whole body had begun to twitch. My hand shook so that I could not hold an electric torch. I who had never been sensitive to cold was about to die of cold. What a strange effect thirst can have!

Somewhere, tired of carrying it in the sun, I had let my waterproof drop. Now the wind was growing bitter and I was learning that in the desert there is no place of refuge. The desert is as smooth as marble. By day it throws no shadow; by night it hands you over naked to the wind. Not a tree, not a hedge, not a rock behind which I could seek shelter. The wind was charging me like a troop of cavalry across open country. I turned and twisted to escape it: I lay down, stood up, lay down again, and still I was exposed to its freezing lash. I had no strength to run from the assassin and under the sabrestroke I tumbled to my knees, my head between my hands.

A little later I pieced these bits together and remembered that I had struggled to my feet and had started to walk on, shivering as I went. I had started forward wondering where I was and then I had heard Prévot. His shouting had jolted me into consciousness.

I went back towards him, still trembling from head to foot—quivering with the attack of hiccups that was convulsing my whole body. To myself I said: "It isn't the cold. It's something else. It's the end." The simple fact was that I hadn't enough water in me. I had tramped too far yesterday and the day before when I was off by myself, and I was dehydrated.

The thought of dying of the cold hurt me. I preferred the phantoms of my mind, the cross, the trees, the lamps. At least they would have killed me by enchantment. But to be whipped to death like a slave! . . .

Confound it! Down on my knees again! We had with us a little store of medicines—a hundred grammes of ninety per cent alcohol, the same of pure ether, and a small bottle of iodine. I tried to swallow a little of the ether: it was like swallowing a knife. Then I tried the alcohol: it contracted my gullet. I dug a pit in the sand, lay down in it, and flung handfuls of sand over me until all but my face was buried in it.

Prévot was able to collect a few twigs, and he lit a fire which soon burnt itself out. He wouldn't bury himself in the sand, but preferred to stamp round and round in a circle. That was foolish.

My throat stayed shut, and though I knew that was a bad sign, I felt better. I felt calm. I felt a peace that was beyond all hope. Once more, despite myself, I was journeying, trussed up on the deck of my slave-ship under the stars. It seemed to me that I was perhaps not in such a bad pass after all.

So long as I lay absolutely motionless, I no longer felt the cold. This allowed me to forget my body buried in the sand. I said to myself that I would not budge an inch, and would therefore never suffer again. As a matter of fact, we really suffer very little. Back of all these torments there is the orchestration of fatigue or of delirium, and we live on in a kind of picture-book, a slightly cruel fairy-tale.

A little while ago the wind had been after me with whip and spur, and I was running in circles like a frightened fox. After that came a time when I couldn't breathe. A great knee was crushing in my chest. A knee. I was writhing in vain to free myself from the weight of the angel who had overthrown me. There had not been a moment when I was alone in this desert. But now I have ceased to believe in my surroundings; I have withdrawn into myself, have shut my eyes, have not so much as batted an eyelid. I have the feeling that this torrent of visions is sweeping me away to a tranquil dream: so rivers cease their turbulence in the embrace of the sea.

Farewell, eyes that I loved! Do not blame me if the

human body cannot go three days without water. I should never have believed that man was so truly the prisoner of the springs and freshets. I had no notion that our self-sufficiency was so circumscribed. We take it for granted that a man is able to stride straight out into the world. We believe that man is free. We never see the cord that binds him to wells and fountains, that umbilical cord by which he is tied to the womb of the world. Let man take but one step too many . . . and the cord snaps.

Apart from your suffering, I have no regrets. All in all, it has been a good life. If I got free of this I should start right in again. A man cannot live a decent life in cities, and I need to feel myself live. I am not thinking of aviation. The airplane is a means, not an end. One doesn't risk one's life for a plane any more than a farmer ploughs for the sake of the plough. But the airplane is a means of getting away from towns and their book-keeping and coming to grips with reality.

Flying is a man's job and its worries are a man's worries. A pilot's business is with the wind, with the stars, with night, with sand, with the sea. He strives to outwit the forces of nature. He stares in expectancy for the coming of dawn the way a gardener awaits the coming of spring. He looks forward to port as to a promised land, and truth for him is what lives in the stars.

I have nothing to complain of. For three days I have tramped the desert, have known the pangs of thirst, have followed false scents in the sand, have pinned my faith on the dew. I have struggled to rejoin my kind, whose very existence on earth I had forgotten. These are the cares of men alive in every fibre, and I cannot help thinking them more important than the fretful choosing of a night-club in which to spend the evening. Compare the one life with the other, and all things considered this is luxury! I have no regrets. I have gambled and lost. It was all in the day's work. At least I have had the unforgettable taste of the sea on my lips.

I am not talking about living dangerously. Such words are meaningless to me. The toreador does not stir me to enthusiasm. It is not danger I love. I know what I love. It is life.

The sky seemed to me faintly bright. I drew up one arm through the sand. There was a bit of the torn parachute within reach, and I ran my hand over it. It was bone dry. Let's see. Dew falls at dawn. Here was dawn risen and no moisture on the cloth. My mind was befuddled and I heard myself say: "There is a dry heart here, a dry heart that cannot know the relief of tears."

I scrambled to my feet. "We're off, Prévot," I said. "Our throats are still open. Get along, man!"

The wind that shrivels up a man in nineteen hours was now blowing out of the west. My gullet was not yet shut, but it was hard and painful and I could feel that there was a rasp in it. Soon that cough would begin that

I had been told about and was now expecting. My tongue was becoming a nuisance. But most serious of all, I was beginning to see shining spots before my eyes. When those spots changed into flames, I should simply lie down.

The first morning hours were cool and we took advantage of them to get on at a good pace. We knew that once the sun was high there would be no more walking for us. We no longer had the right to sweat. Certainly not to stop and catch our breath. This coolness was merely the coolness of low humidity. The prevailing wind was coming from the desert, and under its soft and treacherous caress the blood was being dried out of us.

Our first day's nourishment had been a few grapes. In the next three days each of us ate half an orange and a bit of cake. If we had had anything left now, we couldn't have eaten it because we had no saliva with which to masticate it. But I had stopped being hungry. Thirsty I was, yes, and it seemed to me that I was suffering less from thirst itself than from the effects of thirst. Gullet hard. Tongue like plaster-of-Paris. A rasping in the throat. A horrible taste in the mouth.

All these sensations were new to me, and though I believed water could rid me of them, nothing in my memory associated them with water. Thirst had become more and more a disease and less and less a craving. I began to realize that the thought of water and fruit was now less agonizing than it had been. I was forgetting the radiance of the orange, just as I was forgetting the eyes under the hat-brim. Perhaps I was forgetting everything.

We had sat down after all, but it could not be for long. Nevertheless, it was impossible to go five hundred yards without our legs giving way. To stretch out on the sand would be marvelous—but it could not be.

The landscape had begun to change. Rocky places grew rarer and the sand was now firm beneath our feet. A mile ahead stood dunes and on those dunes we could see a scrubby vegetation. At least this sand was preferable to the steely surface over which we had been trudging. This was the golden desert. This might have been the Sahara. It was in a sense my country.

Two hundred yards had now become our limit, but we had determined to carry on until we reached the vegetation. Better than that we could not hope to do. A week later, when we went back over our traces in a car to have a look at the *Simoon*, I measured this last lap and found that it was just short of fifty miles. All told we had done one hundred and twenty-four miles.

The previous day I had tramped without hope. Today the word "hope" had grown meaningless. Today we were tramping simply because we were tramping. Probably oxen work for the same reason. Yesterday I had dreamed of a paradise of orange-trees. Today I would not give a button for paradise; I did not believe oranges existed. When I thought about myself I found in me nothing but a heart squeezed dry. I was tottering but emotionless. I felt no distress whatever, and in a way I regretted it: misery would have seemed to me as sweet as water. I might then have felt sorry for myself and commiserated with myself as with a friend. But I had not a friend left on earth.

Later, when we were rescued, seeing our burnt-out eyes men thought we must have called aloud and wept and suffered. But cries of despair, misery, sobbing grief are a kind of wealth, and we possessed no wealth. When a young girl is disappointed in love she weeps and knows sorrow. Sorrow is one of the vibrations that prove the fact of living. I felt no sorrow. I was the desert. I could no longer bring up a little saliva; neither could I any longer summon those moving visions towards which I should have loved to stretch forth arms. The sun had dried up the springs of tears in me.

And yet, what was that? A ripple of hope went through me like a faint breeze over a lake. What was this sign that had awakened my instinct before knocking on the door of my consciousness? Nothing had changed, and yet everything was changed. This sheet of sand, these low hummocks and sparse tufts of verdure that had been a landscape, were now become a stage setting. Thus far the stage was empty, but the scene was set. I looked at Prévot. The same astonishing thing had happened to him as to me, but he was as far from guessing its significance as I was.

I swear to you that something is about to happen. I swear that life has sprung in this desert. I swear that this emptiness, this stillness, has suddenly become more stirring than a tumult on a public square.

"Prévot! Footprints! We are saved!"

We had wandered from the trail of the human species; we had cast ourselves forth from the tribe; we had found ourselves alone on earth and forgotten by the universal migration; and here, imprinted in the sand, were the divine and naked feet of man!

"Look, Prévot, here two men stood together and then separated."

"Here a camel knelt."

"Here . . ."

But it was not true that we were already saved. It was not enough to squat down and wait. Before long we should be past saving. Once the cough has begun, the progress made by thirst is swift.

Still, I believed in that caravan swaying somewhere in the desert, heavy with its cargo of treasure.

We went on. Suddenly I heard a cock crow. I remembered what Guillaumet had told me: "Towards the end I heard cocks crowing in the Andes. And I heard the railway train." The instant the cock crowed I thought of Guillaumet and I said to myself: "First it was my eyes that played tricks on me. I suppose this is another of the effects of thirst. Probably my ears have merely held out longer than my eyes." But Prévot grabbed my arm:

"Did you hear that?"

"What?"

"The cock."

"Why . . . why, yes, I did."

To myself I said: "Fool! Get it through your head! This means life!"

I had one last hallucination—three dogs chasing one another. Prévot looked, but could not see them. However, both of us waved our arms at a Bedouin. Both of us shouted with all the breath in our bodies, and laughed for happiness.

But our voices could not carry thirty yards. The Bedouin on his slow-moving camel had come into view from behind a dune and now he was moving slowly out of sight. The man was probably the only Arab in this desert, sent by a demon to materialize and vanish before the eyes of us who could not run.

We saw in profile on the dune another Arab. We shouted, but our shouts were whispers. We waved our arms and it seemed to us that they must fill the sky with monstrous signals. Still the Bedouin stared with averted face away from us.

At last, slowly, slowly he began a right angle turn in our direction. At the very second when he came face to face with us, I thought, the curtain would come down.

At the very second when his eyes met ours, thirst would vanish and by this man would death and the mirages be wiped out. Let this man but make a quarter-turn left and the world is changed. Let him but bring his torso round, but sweep the scene with a glance, and like a god he can create life.

The miracle had come to pass. He was walking towards us over the sand like a god over the waves.

The Arab looked at us without a word. He placed his hands upon our shoulders and we obeyed him: we stretched out upon the sand. Race, language, religion were forgotten. There was only this humble nomad with the hands of an archangel on our shoulders.

Face to the sand, we waited. And when the water came, we drank like calves with our faces in the basin, and with a greediness which alarmed the Bedouin so that from time to time he pulled us back. But as soon as his hand fell away from us we plunged our faces anew into the water.

Water, thou hast no taste, no color, no odor; canst not be defined, art relished while ever mysterious. Not necessary to life, but rather life itself, thou fillest us with a gratification that exceeds the delight of the senses. By thy might, there return into us treasures that we had abandoned. By thy grace, there are released in us all the dried-up runnels of our heart. Of the riches that exist in the world, thou art the rarest and also the most delicate—thou so pure within the bowels of the earth! A man may die of thirst lying beside a magnesian spring. He may die within reach of a salt lake. He may die though he hold in his hand a jug of dew, if it be inhabited by evil salts. For thou, water, art a proud divinity, allowing no alteration, no foreignness in thy being. And the joy that thou spreadest is an infinitely simple joy.

You, Bedouin of Libya who saved our lives, though you will dwell for ever in my memory yet I shall never be able to recapture your features. You are Humanity and your face comes into my mind simply as man incarnate. You, our beloved fellowman, did not know who we might be, and yet you recognized us without fail. And I, in my turn, shall recognize you in the faces of all mankind. You came towards me in an aureole of charity and magnanimity bearing the gift of water. All my friends and all my enemies marched towards me in your person. It did not seem to me that you were rescuing me: rather did it seem that you were forgiving me. And I felt I had no enemy left in all the world.

This is the end of my story. Lifted on to a camel, we went on for three hours. Then, broken with weariness, we asked to be set down at a camp while the cameleers went on ahead for help. Towards six in the evening a car manned by armed Bedouins came to fetch us. A half-hour later we were set down at the house of a Swiss engineer named Raccaud who was operating a soda factory beside saline deposits in the desert. He was unforgettably kind to us. By midnight we were in Cairo.

I awoke between white sheets. Through the curtains came the rays of a sun that was no longer an enemy. I spread butter and honey on my bread. I smiled. I recaptured the savor of my childhood and all its marvels. And I read and re-read the telegram from those dearest to me in all the world whose three words had shattered me:

"So terribly happy!"

· 9 ·

Barcelona and Madrid
(1936)

ONCE again I had found myself in the presence of a truth and had failed to recognize it. Consider what had happened to me: I had thought myself lost, had touched the very bottom of despair; and then, when the spirit of renunciation had filled me, I had known peace. I know now what I was not conscious of at the time—that in such an hour a man feels that he has finally found himself and has become his own friend. An essential inner need has been satisfied, and against that satisfaction, that self-fulfilment, no external power can prevail. Bonnafous, I imagine, he who spent his life

racing before the wind, was acquainted with this serenity of spirit. Guillaumet, too, in his snows. Never shall
I forget that, lying buried to the chin in sand, strangled
slowly to death by thirst, my heart was infinitely warm
beneath the desert stars.

What can men do to make known to themselves this
sense of deliverance? Everything about mankind is para-
dox. He who strives and conquers grows soft. The mag-
nanimous man grown rich becomes mean. The creative
artist for whom everything is made easy nods. Every
doctrine swears that it can breed men, but none can tell
us in advance what sort of men it will breed. Men are
not cattle to be fattened for market. In the scales of life
an indigent Newton weighs more than a parcel of pros-
perous nonentities. All of us have had the experience of
a sudden joy that came when nothing in the world had
forewarned us of its coming—a joy so thrilling that if it
was born of misery we remembered even the misery with
tenderness. All of us, on seeing old friends again, have
remembered with happiness the trials we lived through
with those friends. Of what can we be certain except
this—that we are fertilized by mysterious circumstances?
Where is man's truth to be found?

Truth is not that which can be demonstrated by the
aid of logic. If orange-trees are hardy and rich in fruit in
this bit of soil and not that, then this bit of soil is what
is truth for orange-trees. If a particular religion, or culture, or scale of values, if one form of activity rather

than another, brings self-fulfilment to a man, releases the prince asleep within him unknown to himself, then that scale of values, that culture, that form of activity, constitute his truth. Logic, you say? Let logic wangle its own explanation of life.

Because it is man and not flying that concerns me most, I shall close this book with the story of man's gropings towards self-fulfilment as I witnessed them in the early months of the civil war in Spain. One year after crashing in the desert I made a tour of the Catalan front in order to learn what happens to man when the scaffolding of his traditions suddenly collapses. To Madrid I went for an answer to another question: How does it happen that men are sometimes willing to die?

I

Flying west from Lyon, I veered left in the direction of the Pyrenees and Spain. Below me floated fleecy white clouds, summer clouds, clouds made for amateur flyers in which great gaps opened like skylights. Through one of these windows I could see Perpignan lying at the bottom of a well of light.

I was flying solo, and as I looked down on Perpignan I was day-dreaming. I had spent six months there once while serving as test pilot at a near-by airdrome. When the day's work was done I would drive into this town where every day was as peaceful as Sunday. I would sit in a wicker chair within sound of the café band, sip a glass of port, and look idly on at the provincial life of the place, reflecting that it was as innocent as a review of lead soldiers. These pretty girls, these carefree strollers, this pure sky. . . .

But here came the Pyrenees. The last happy town was left behind.

Below me lay Figueras, and Spain. This was where men killed one another. What was most astonishing here was not the sight of conflagration, ruin, and signs of man's distress—it was the absence of all these. Figueras seemed no different from Perpignan. I leaned out and stared hard.

There were no scars on that heap of white gravel, that church gleaming in the sun, which I knew had been burnt. I could not distinguish its irreparable wounds. Gone was the pale smoke that had carried off its gilding, had melted in the blue of the sky its altar screens, its prayer books, its sacerdotal treasures. Not a line of the church was altered. This town, seated at the heart of its fan-shaped roads like a spider at the centre of its silken trap, looked very much like the other.

Like other towns, this one was nourished by the fruits of the plain that rose along the white highways to meet it. All that I could discern was the slow gnawing which, through the centuries, had swallowed up the soil, driven away the forests, divided up the fields, dug out these life-giving irrigation ditches. Here was a face

unlikely to change much, for it was already old. A colony of bees, I said to myself, once it was established so
solidly within the boundaries of an acre of flowers,
would be assured of peace. But peace is not given to a
colony of men.

Human drama does not show itself on the surface of
life. It is not played out in the visible world, but in the
hearts of men. Even in happy Perpignan a victim of
cancer walled up behind his hospital window goes round
and round in a circle striving helplessly to escape the
pain that hovers over him like a relentless kite. One man
in misery can disrupt the peace of a city. It is another
of the miraculous things about mankind that there is no
pain nor passion that does not radiate to the ends of
the earth. Let a man in a garret but burn with enough
intensity and he will set fire to the world.

Gerona went by, Barcelona loomed into view, and I
let myself glide gently down from the perch of my
observatory. Even here I could see nothing out of the
way, unless it was that the avenues were deserted.
Again there were devastated churches which, from
above, looked untouched. Faintly visible was something
that I guessed to be smoke. Was that one of the signs I
was seeking? Was this a scrap of evidence of that nearly
soundless anger whose all-destroying wrath was so hard
to measure? A whole civilization was contained in that
faint golden puff so lightly dispersed by a breath of
wind.

I am quite convinced of the sincerity of people who say: "Terror in Barcelona? Nonsense. That great city in ashes? A mere twenty houses wrecked. Streets heaped with the dead? A few hundred killed out of a population of a million. Where did you see a firing line running with blood and deafening with the roar of guns?"

I agree that I saw no firing line. I saw groups of tranquil men and women strolling on the Ramblas. When, on occasion, I ran against a barricade of militiamen in arms, a smile was often enough to open the way before me. I did not come at once upon the firing line. In a civil war the firing line is invisible; it passes through the hearts of men. And yet, on my very first night in Barcelona I skirted it.

I was sitting on the pavement of a café, sipping my drink surrounded by light-hearted men and women, when suddenly four armed men stopped where I sat, stared at a man at the next table, and without a word pointed their guns at his stomach. Streaming with sweat the man stood up and raised leaden arms above his head. One of the militiamen ran his hands over his clothes and his eyes over some papers he found in the man's pockets, and ordered him to come along.

The man left his half-emptied glass, the last glass of his life, and started down the road. Surrounded by the squad, his hands stuck up like the hands of a man going down for the last time.

"Fascist!" A woman behind me said it with contempt.

She was the only witness who dared betray that anything out of the ordinary had taken place. Untouched, the man's glass stood on the table, a mute witness to a mad confidence in chance, in forgiveness, in life. I sat watching the disappearance in a ring of rifles of a man who five minutes before, within two feet of me, had crossed the invisible firing line.

My guides were anarchists. They led me to the railway station where troops were being entrained. Far from the platforms built for tender farewells, we were walking in a desert of signal towers and switching points, stumbling in the rain through a labyrinthine yard filled with blackened goods wagons where tarpaulins the color of lard were spread over carloads of stiffened forms. This world had lost its human quality, had become a world of iron, and therefore uninhabitable. A ship remains a living thing only so long as man with his brushes and oils swabs an artificial layer of light over it. Leave them to themselves a couple of weeks and the life dies out of your ship, your factory, your railway; death covers their faces. After six thousand years the stones of a temple still vibrate with the passage of man; but a little rust, a night of rain, and this railway yard is eaten away to its very skeleton.

Here are our men. Cannon and machine-guns are being loaded on board with the straining muscles and the hoarse gaspings that are always drawn from men by these monstrous insects, these fleshless insects, these lumps of carapace and vertebra. What is startling here is the silence. Not a note of song, not a single shout. Only, now and then, when a gun-carriage lands, the hollow thump of a steel plate. Of human voices no sound.

No uniforms, either. These men are going off to be killed in their working garb. Wearing their dark clothes stiff with mud, the column heaving and sweating at their work look like the denizens of a night shelter. They fill me with the same uneasiness I felt when the yellow fever broke out among us at Dakar, ten years ago.

The chief of the detachment had been speaking to me in a whisper. I caught the end of his speech:

". . . and we move up to Saragossa."

Why the devil did he have to whisper! The atmosphere of this yard made me think of a hospital. But of course! That was it. A civil war is not a war, it is a disease. These men were not going up to the front in the exultation of certain victory; they were struggling blindly against infection.

And the same thing was going on in the enemy camp. The purpose of this struggle was not to rid the country of an invading foreigner but to eradicate a plague. A new faith is like a plague. It attacks from within. It propagates in the invisible. Walking in the streets, whoever belongs to a Party feels himself surrounded by secretly infected men.

This must have been why these troops were going

off in silence with their instruments of asphyxiation. There was not the slightest resemblance between them and regiments that go into battle against foreign armies and are set out on the chessboard of the fields and moved about by strategists. These men had gathered together haphazardly in a city filled with chaos.

There was not much to choose between Barcelona and its enemy, Saragossa: both were composed of the same swarm of communists, anarchists, and fascists. The very men who collected on the same side were perhaps more different from one another than from their enemies. In civil war the enemy is inward; one as good as fights against oneself.

What else can explain the particular horror of this war in which firing squads count for more than soldiers of the line? Death in this war is a sort of quarantine. Purges take place of germ-carriers. The anarchists go from house to house and load the plague-stricken into their tumbrils, while on the other side of the barricade Franco is able to utter that horrible boast: "There are no more communists among us."

The conscripts are weeded out by a kind of medical board; the officer in charge is a sort of army doctor. Men present themselves for service with pride shining in their eyes and the belief in their hearts that they have a part to play in society.

"Exempt from service for life!" is the decision.

Fields have been turned into charnel-houses and the

dead are burned in lime or petroleum. Respect for the dignity of man has been trampled under foot. Since on both sides the political parties spy upon the stirrings of man's conscience as upon the workings of a disease, why should the urn of his flesh be respected? This body that clothes the spirit, that moves with grace and boldness, that knows love, that is apt for self-sacrifice—no one now so much as thinks of giving it decent burial.

I thought of our respect for the dead. I thought of the white sanatorium where the light of a man's life goes quietly out in the presence of those who love him and who garner as if it were an inestimable treasure his last words, his ultimate smile. How right they are! Seeing that this same whole is never again to take shape in the world. Never again will be heard exactly that note of laughter, that intonation of voice, that quality of repartee. Each individual is a miracle. No wonder we go on speaking of the dead for twenty years.

Here, in Spain, a man is simply stood up against a wall and he gives up his entrails to the stones of the courtyard. You have been captured. You are shot. Reason: your ideas were not our ideas.

This entrainment in the rain is the only thing that rings true about their war. These men stand round and stare at me, and I read in their eyes a mournful sobriety. They know the fate that awaits them if they are captured. I begin to shiver with the cold and observe of a sudden that no woman has been allowed to see them off.

The absence of women seems to me right. There is no place here for mothers who bring children into the world in ignorance of the faith that will some day flare up in their sons, in ignorance of the ideologist who, according to his lights, will prop up their sons against a wall when they have come to their twenty years of life.

We went up by motor into the war zone. Barricades became more frequent, and from place to place we had to negotiate with revolutionary committees. Passes were valid only from one village to the next.

"Are you trying to get closer to the front?"

"Exactly."

The chairman of the local committee consulted a large-scale map.

"You won't be able to get through. The rebels have occupied the road four miles ahead. But you might try swinging left here. This road ought to be free. Though there was talk of rebel cavalry cutting it this morning."

It was very difficult in those early days of the revolution to know one's way about in the vicinity of the front. There were loyal villages, rebel villages, neutral villages, and they shifted their allegiance between dawn and dark. This tangle of loyal and rebel zones made me think the push must be pretty weak. It certainly bore no resemblance to a line of trenches cutting off friend from enemy as cleanly as a knife. I felt as if I were walking in a bog. Here the earth was solid beneath our feet: there we sank into it. We moved in a maze of uncertainty. Yet what space, what air between movements! These military operations are curiously lacking in density.

Once again we reached a point beyond which we were told we could not advance. Six rifles and a low wall of paving stones blocked the road. Four men and two women lay stretched on the ground behind the wall. I made a mental note that the women did not know how to hold a rifle.

"This is as far as you can go."

"Why?"

"Rebels."

We got out of the car and sat down with the militiamen upon the grass. They put down their rifles and cut a few slices of fresh bread.

"Is this your village?" we asked.

"No, we are Catalans, from Barcelona. Communist Party."

One of the girls stretched herself and sat up on the barricade, her hair blowing in the wind. She was rather thick-set, but young and healthy. Smiling happily she said:

"I am going to stay in this village when the war is over. I didn't know it, but the country beats the city all hollow."

She cast a loving glance round at the countryside, as

if stirred by a revelation. Her life had been the gray slums, days spent in a factory, and the sordid compensation afforded by the cafés. Everything that went on here seemed to her as jolly as a picnic. She jumped down and ran to the village well. Probably she believed she was drinking at the very breast of mother earth.

"Have you done any fighting here?"

"No. The rebels kick up a little dust now and then, but . . . We see a lorryload of men from time to time and hope that they will come along this road. But nothing has come by in two weeks."

They were awaiting their first enemy. In the rebel village opposite sat another half-dozen militiamen awaiting a first enemy. Twelve warriors alone in the world.

Each side was waiting for something to be born in the invisible. The rebels were waiting for the host of hesitant people in Madrid to declare themselves for Franco. Barcelona was waiting for Saragossa to waken out of an inspired dream, declare itself Socialist, and fall. It was the thought more than the soldier that was besieging the town. The thought was the great hope and the great enemy.

It seemed to me that the bombers, the shells, the militiamen under arms, by themselves had no power to conquer. On each side a single man entrenched behind his line of defense was better than a hundred besiegers. But thought might worm its way in.

From time to time there is an attack. From time to

time the tree is shaken. Not to uproot it, but merely to see if the fruit is yet ripe. And if it is, a town falls.

II

Back from the front, I found friends in Barcelona who allowed me to join in their mysterious expeditions. We went deep into the mountains and were now in one of those villages which are possessed by a mixture of peace and terror.

"Oh, yes, we shot seventeen of them."

They had shot seventeen "fascists." The parish priest, the priest's housekeeper, the sexton, and fourteen village notables. Everything is relative, you see. When they read in their provincial newspaper the story of the life of Basil Zaharoff, master of the world, they transpose it into their own language. They recognize in him the nurseryman, or the pharmacist. And when they shoot the pharmacist, in a way they are shooting Basil Zaharoff. The only one who does not understand is the pharmacist.

"Now we are all Loyalists together. Everything has calmed down."

Almost everything. The conscience of the village is tormented by one man whom I have seen at the tavern, smiling, helpful, so anxious to go on living! He comes to the pub in order to show us that, despite his few acres of vineyard, he too is part of the human race, suffers with rheumatism like it, mops his face like it with a blue handkerchief. He comes, and he plays billiards. Can one shoot a man who plays billiards? Besides, he plays badly with his great trembling hands. He is upset; he still does not know whether he is a fascist or not. He puts me in mind of those poor monkeys who dance before the boa-constrictor in the hope of softening it.

There was nothing we could do for the man. For the time being we had another job in hand. Sitting on a table and swinging my legs at committee headquarters, while my companion, Pépin, pulled a bundle of soiled papers out of his pocket, I had a good look at these terrorists. Their looks belied their name: honorable peasants with frank eyes and sober attentive faces, they were the same everywhere we went; and though we were foreigners possessing no authority, we were everywhere received with the same grave courtesy.

"Yes, here it is," said Pépin, a document in his hand. "His name is Laporte. Any of you know him?"

The paper went from hand to hand and the members of the committee shook their heads.

"No. Laporte? Never heard of him."

I started to explain something to them, but Pépin motioned me to be silent. "They won't talk," he said, "but they know him well enough."

Pépin spread his references before the chairman, saying casually:

"I am a French socialist. Here is my party card."

The card was passed round and the chairman raised his eyes to us:

"Laporte. I don't believe. . . ."

"Of course you know him. A French monk. Probably in disguise. You captured him yesterday in the woods. Laporte, his name is. The French consulate wants him."

I sat swinging my legs. What a strange session! Here we were in a mountain village sixty miles from the French frontier, asking a revolutionary committee that shot even parish priests' housekeepers to surrender to us in good shape a French monk. Whatever happened to us, we would certainly have asked for it. Nevertheless, I felt safe. There was no treachery in these people. And why, as a matter of fact, should they bother to play tricks? We had absolutely no protection; we meant no more to them than Laporte; they could do anything they pleased.

Pépin nudged me. "I've an idea we have come too late," he said.

The chairman cleared his throat and made up his mind.

"This morning," he said, "we found a dead man on the road just outside the village. He must be there still."

And he pretended to send off for the dead man's papers.

"They've already shot him," Pépin said to me. "Too

bad! They would certainly have turned him over to us.
They are good kind people."

I looked straight into the eyes of these curious "good
kind people." Strange: there was nothing in their eyes to
upset me. There seemed nothing to fear in their set jaws
and the blank smoothness of their faces. Blank, as if
vaguely bored. A rather terrible blankness. I wondered
why, despite our unusual mission, we were not suspect
to them. What difference had they established in their
minds between us and the "fascist" in the neighboring
tavern who was dancing his dance of death before the
unavailing indifference of these judges? A crazy notion
came into my head, forced upon my attention by all
the power of my instinct: If one of those men yawned
I should be afraid. I should feel that all human com-
munication had snapped between us.

After we left, I said to Pépin:

"That is the third village in which we have done this
job and I still cannot make up my mind whether the
job is dangerous or not."

Pépin laughed and admitted that although he had
saved dozens of men on these missions, he himself did
not know the answer.

"Yesterday," he confessed, "I had a narrow squeak.
I snaffled a Carthusian monk away from them just as
they were about to shoot the fellow. The smell of blood
was in the air, and . . . Well, they growled a bit, you
know."

I know the end of that story. Pépin, the socialist and notorious anti-church political worker, having staked his life to get that Carthusian, had hustled him into a motor-car and there, by way of compensation, he sought to insult the priest by the finest bit of blasphemy he could summon:

"You . . . you . . . you triple damned monk!" he had finally spluttered.

This was Pépin's triumph. But the monk, who had not been listening, flung his arms round Pépin's neck and wept with happiness.

In another village they gave up a man to us. With a great air of mystery, four militiamen dug him up out of a cellar. He was a lively bright-eyed monk whose name I have already forgotten, disguised as a peasant and carrying a long gnarled stick scarred with notches.

"I kept track of the days," he explained. "Three weeks in the woods is a long time. Mushrooms are not specially nourishing, and they grabbed me when I came near a village."

The mayor of the village, to whom we owed this gift, was very proud of him.

"We shot at him a lot and thought we had killed him," he said. And then, by way of excuse for the bad marksmanship, he added: "I must say it was at night."

The monk laughed.

"I wasn't afraid."

We put him into the car, and before we threw in the

clutch everybody had to shake hands all round with these terrible terrorists. The monk's hand was shaken hardest of all and he was repeatedly congratulated on being alive. To all these friendly sentiments he responded with a warmth of unquestionably sincere appreciation.

As for me, I wish I understood mankind.

We went over our lists. At Sitges lived a man who, we had been told, was in danger of being shot. We drove round and found his door wide open. Up a flight of stairs we ran into our skinny young man.

"It seems that these people are likely to shoot you," we told him. "Come back to Barcelona with us and you will be shipped home to France in the *Duquesne*."

The young man took a long time to think this over and then said:

"This is some trick of my sister's."

"What?"

"She lives in Barcelona. She would never pay for the child's keep and I always had to. . . ."

"Your family troubles are none of our affair. Are you in danger here, yes or no?"

"I don't know. I tell you, my sister . . ."

"Do you want to get away, yes or no?"

"I really don't know. What do you think? In Barcelona, my sister . . ."

The man was carrying on his family quarrel through

the revolution. He was going to stay here in order to do his sister in the eye.

"Do as you please," we said, finally, and we left him where he was.

We stopped the car and got out. A volley of rifle-shot had crackled in the still country air. From the top of the road we looked down upon a clump of trees out of which, a quarter of a mile away, stuck two tall chimneys. A squad of militiamen came up and loaded their guns. We asked what was going on. They looked round, pointed to the chimneys, and decided that the firing must have come from the factory.

The shooting died down almost immediately, and silence fell again. The chimneys went on smoking peacefully. A ripple of wind ran over the grass. Nothing had changed visibly, and we ourselves were unchanged. Nevertheless, in that clump of trees someone had just died.

One of the militiamen said that a girl had been killed at the factory, together with her brothers, but there was still some uncertainty about this. What excruciating simplicity! Our own peace of mind had not been invaded by those muffled sounds in the clump of greenery, by that brief partridge drive. The angelus, as it were, that had rung out in that foliage had left us calm and unrepentant.

Human events display two faces, one of drama and

the other of indifference. Everything changes according as the event concerns the individual or the species. In its migrations, in its imperious impulses, the species forgets its dead. This, perhaps, explains the unperturbed faces of these peasants. One feels that they have no special taste for horror; yet they will come back from that clump of trees on the one hand content to have administered their kind of justice, and on the other hand quite indifferent to the fate of the girl who stumbled against the root of the tree of death, who was caught by death's harpoon as she fled, and who now lies in the wood, her mouth filled with blood.

Here I touch the inescapable contradiction I shall never be able to resolve. For man's greatness does not reside merely in the destiny of the species: each individual is an empire. When a mine caves in and closes over the head of a single miner, the life of the community is suspended.

His comrades, their women, their children, gather in anguish at the entrance to the mine, while below them the rescue party scratch with their picks at the bowels of the earth. What are they after? Are they consciously saving one unit of society? Are they freeing a human being as one might free a horse, after computing the work he is still capable of doing? Ten other miners may be killed in the attempted rescue: what inept cost accounting! Of course it is not a matter of saving one ant out of the colony of ants! They are rescuing a consciousness, an empire whose significance is incommensurable with anything else.

Inside the narrow skull of the miner pinned beneath the fallen timber, there lives a world. Parents, friends, a home, the hot soup of evening, songs sung on feast days, loving kindness and anger, perhaps even a social consciousness and a great universal love, inhabit that skull. By what are we to measure the value of a man? His ancestor once drew a reindeer on the wall of a cave; and two hundred thousand years later that gesture still radiates. It stirs us, prolongs itself in us. Man's gestures are an eternal spring. Though we die for it, we shall bring up that miner from his shaft. Solitary he may be; universal he surely is.

In Spain there are crowds in movement, but the individual, that universe, calls in vain for help from the bottom of the mine.

III

Machine-gun bullets cracked against the stone above our heads as we skirted the moonlit wall. Low-flying lead thudded into the rubble of an embankment that rose on the other side of the road. Half a mile away a battle was in progress, the line of fire drawn in the shape of a horse-shoe ahead of us and on our flanks.

Walking between wall and parapet on the white highway, my guide and I were able to disregard the spattel of missiles in a feeling of perfect security. We could sing, we could laugh, we could strike matches, without drawing upon ourselves the direct fire of the enemy. We went forward like peasants on their way to market. Half a mile away the iron hand of war would have set us inescapably upon the black chessboard of battle; but here, out of the game, ignored, the Republican lieutenant and I were as free as air.

Shells filled the night with absurd parabolas during their three seconds of freedom between release and exhaustion. There were the duds that dove without bursting into the ground; there were the travelers in space that whipped straight overhead, elongated in their race to the stars. And the leaden bullets that ricocheted in our faces and tinkled curiously in our ears were like bees, dangerous for the twinkling of an eye, poisonous but ephemeral.

Walking on, we reached a point where the embankment had collapsed.

"We might follow the cross-trench from here," my guide suggested.

Things had suddenly turned serious. Not that we were in the line of machine-gun fire, or that a roving searchlight was about to spot us. It was not as bad as that. There had simply been a rustling overhead; a sort of celestial gurgle had sounded. It meant no harm to us, but the lieutenant remarked suddenly, "That is meant for Madrid," and we went down into the trench.

The trench ran along the crest of a hill a little before reaching the suburb of Carabanchel. In the direction of Madrid a part of the parapet had crumbled and we could see the city in the gap, white, strangely white, under the full moon. Hardly a mile separated us from those tall structures dominated by the tower of the Telephone Building.

Madrid was asleep—or rather Madrid was feigning sleep. Not a light; not a sound. Like clockwork, every two minutes the funereal fracas that we were henceforth to hear roared forth and was dissolved in a dead silence. It seemed to waken no sound and no stirring in the city, but was swallowed up each time like a stone in water.

Suddenly in the place of Madrid I felt that I was staring at a face with closed eyes. The hard face of an obstinate virgin taking blow after blow without a moan. Once again there sounded overhead that gurgling in the stars of a newly uncorked bottle. One second, two seconds, five seconds went by. There was an explosion and I ducked involuntarily. There goes the whole town, I thought.

But Madrid was still there. Nothing had collapsed. Not an eye had blinked. Nothing was changed. The stone face was as pure as ever.

"Meant for Madrid," the lieutenant repeated mechanically. He taught me to tell these celestial shudders apart, to follow the course of these sharks rushing upon their prey:

"No, that is one of our batteries replying. . . . That's theirs, but firing somewhere else. . . . There's one meant for Madrid."

Waiting for an explosion is the longest passage of time I know. What things go on in that interminable moment! An enormous pressure rises, rises. Will that boiler ever make up its mind to burst? At last! For some that meant death, but there are others for whom it meant escape from death. Eight hundred thousand souls, less half a score of dead, have won a last-minute reprieve. Between the gurgling and the explosion eight hundred thousand lives were in danger of death.

Each shell in the air threatened them all. I could feel the city out there, tense, compact, a solid. I saw them all in the mind's eye—men, women, children, all that humble population crouching in the sheltering cloak of stone of a motionless virgin. Again I heard the ignoble crash and was gripped and sickened by the downward course of the torpedo. . . . Torpedo? I scarcely knew what I was saying. "They . . . they are torpedoing Madrid." And the lieutenant, standing there counting the shells, said:

"Meant for Madrid. Sixteen."

I crept out of the trench, lay flat on my stomach on the parapet, and stared. A new image has wiped out the old. Madrid with its chimney-pots, its towers, its port-holes, now looks like a ship on the high seas. Madrid all white on the black waters of the night. A city outlives its inhabitants. Madrid, loaded with emigrants, is ferrying them from one shore to the other of life. It has a generation on board. Slowly it navigates through the centuries. Men, women, children fill it from garret to hold. Resigned or quaking with fear, they live only for the moment to come. A vessel loaded with humanity is being torpedoed. The purpose of the enemy is to sink Madrid as if she were a ship.

Stretched out on the parapet I do not care a curse for the rules of war. For justifications or for motives. I listen. I have learned to read the course of these gurglings among the stars. They pass quite close to Sagittarius. I have learned to count slowly up to five. And I listen. But what tree has been sundered by this lightning, what cathedral has been gutted, what poor child has just been stricken, I have no means of knowing.

That same afternoon I had witnessed a bombardment in the town itself. All the force of this thunder-clap had to burst on the Gran Via in order to uproot a human life. One single life. Passers-by had brushed rubbish off their clothes; others had scattered on the run; and when the light smoke had risen and cleared away, the betrothed, escaped by miracle without a scratch, found at his feet his *novia*, whose golden arm a moment before had been in his, changed into a blood-filled sponge, changed into a limp packet of flesh and rags.

He had knelt down, still uncomprehending, had

nodded his head slowly, as if saying to himself, "Something very strange has happened."

This marvel spattered on the pavement bore no resemblance to what had been his beloved. Misery was excruciatingly slow to engulf him in its tidal wave. For still another second, stunned by the feat of the invisible prestidigitator, he cast a bewildered glance round him in search of the slender form, as if it at least should have survived. Nothing was there but a packet of muck.

Gone was the feeble spark of humanity. And while in the man's throat there was brewing that shriek which I know not what deferred, he had the leisure to reflect that it was not those lips he had loved but their pout, not them but their smile. Not those eyes, but their glance. Not that breast, but its gentle swell. He was free to discover at last the source of the anguish love had been storing up for him, to learn that it was the unattainable he had been pursuing. What he had yearned to embrace was not the flesh but a downy spirit, a spark, the impalpable angel that inhabits the flesh.

I do not care a curse for the rules of war and the law of reprisal. As for the military advantage of such a bombardment, I simply cannot grasp it. I have seen housewives disemboweled, children mutilated; I have seen the old itinerant market crone sponge from her treasures the brains with which they were spattered. I have seen a janitor's wife come out of her cellar and douse the sullied pavement with a bucket of water, and I am still unable to understand what part these humble slaughter-house accidents play in warfare.

A moral rôle? But a bombardment turns against the bombarder! Each shell that fell upon Madrid fortified something in the town. It persuaded the hesitant neutral to plump for the defenders. A dead child weighs heavily in the balance when it is one's own. It was clear to me that a bombardment did not disperse—it unified. Horror causes men to clench their fists, and in horror men join together.

The lieutenant and I crawled along the parapet. Face or ship, Madrid stood erect, receiving blows without a moan. But men are like this: slowly but surely, ordeal fortifies their virtues.

Because of the ordeal my companion's heart was high. He was thinking of the hardening of Madrid's will. He stood up with his fists on his hips, breathing heavily. Pity for the women and the children had gone out of him.

"That makes sixty," he counted grimly.

The blow resounded on the anvil. A giant smith was forging Madrid.

One side or the other would win. Madrid would resist or it would fall. A thousand forces were engaged in this mortal confusion of tongues from which anything might come forth. But one did not need to be a Martian, did not need to see these men dispassionately in a long perspective, in order to perceive that they were struggling against themselves, were their own enemy. Mankind perhaps was being brought to bed of something here in Spain; something perhaps was to be born of this chaos, this disruption. For indeed not all that I saw in Spain was horror, not all of it filled my mouth with a taste of ashes.

IV

On the Guadalajara front I sat at night in a dugout with a Republican squad made up of a lieutenant, a sergeant, and three men. They were about to go out on patrol duty. One of them—the night was cold—stood half in shadow with his head not quite through the neck of a sweater he was pulling on, his arms caught in the sleeves and waving slowly and awkwardly in the air like the short arms of a bear. Smothered curses, stubbles of beard, distant muffled explosions—the atmosphere was a strange compound of sleep, waking, and death. I thought of tramps on the road bestirring themselves, raising themselves up off the ground on heavy sticks. Caught in the earth, painted by the earth, their hands grubby with their gardenless gardening, these men were raising themselves painfully out of the mud in order to emerge under the stars. In these blocks of caked clay I could sense the awakening of consciousness, and as I looked at them I said to myself that across the way, at

this very moment, the enemy was getting into his harness, was thickening his body with woolen sweaters;
earth-crusted, he was breaking out of his mould of hardened mud. Across the way the same clay shaping the
same beings was wakening in the same way into consciousness.

The patrol moved forward across fields through
crackling stubble, knocking its toes against unseen rocks
in the dark. We were making our way down into a
narrow valley on the other side of which the enemy
was entrenched. Caught in the cross-fire of artillery,
the peasants had evacuated this valley, and their deserted
village lay here drowned in the waters of war. Only
their dogs remained, ghostly creatures that hunted their
pitiful prey in the day and howled in the night. At four
in the morning, when the moon rose white as a picked
bone, a whole village bayed at the dead divinity.

"Go down and find out if the enemy is hiding in that
village," the commanding officer had ordered. Very
likely on the other side the same order had been given.

We were accompanied by a sort of political agent, a
civilian, whose name I have forgotten, though not what
he looked like. It seems to me he must have been rheu-
matic, and I remember that he leaned heavily on a
knotted stick as we tramped forward in the night. His
face was the face of a conscientious and elderly work-
man. I would have sworn that he was above politics and
parties, above ideological rivalries. "Pity it is," he would

say, "that as things are we cannot explain our point of view to the other fellow." He walked weighed down by his doctrine, like an evangelist. Across the way, meanwhile, was the other evangelist, a believer just as enlightened as this one, his boots just as muddy, his duty taking him on exactly the same errand.

"You'll hear them pretty soon," my commissar said. "When we get close enough we'll call out to the enemy, ask him questions; and he may answer tonight."

Although we don't yet know it, we are in search of a gospel to embrace all gospels, we are on the march towards a stormy Sinai.

And we have arrived. Here is a dazed sentry, half asleep in the shadow of a stone wall.

"Yes," says my commissar, "sometimes they answer. Sometimes they call out first and ask questions. Of course they don't answer, too, sometimes. Depends on the mood they're in."

Just like the gods.

A hundred yards behind us lie our trenches. I strike a match, intending to light a cigarette, and two powerful hands duck my head. Everybody has ducked, and I hear the whistle of bullets in the air. Then silence. The shots were fired high and the volley was not repeated— a mere reminder from the enemy of what constitutes decorum here. One does not light a cigarette in the face of the enemy.

We are joined by three or four men, wrapped in blankets, who had been posted behind neighboring walls.

"Looks as if the lads across the way were awake," one of them remarks.

"Do you think they'll talk tonight? We'd like to talk to them."

"One of them, Antonio, he talks sometimes."

"Call him."

The man in the blanket straightens up, cups his hands round his mouth, takes a deep breath, and calls out slowly and loudly: "An . . . to . . . ni . . . o!"

The call swells, unfurls, floats across the valley and echoes back.

"Better duck," my neighbor advises. "Sometimes when you call them, they let fly."

Crouched behind the stone wall, we listen. No sound of a shot. Yet we cannot say we have heard nothing at all, for the whole night is singing like a sea-shell.

"Hi! Antonio . . . o! Are you . . ."

The man in the blanket draws another deep breath and goes on:

"Are you asleep?"

"Asleep?" says the echo. "Asleep?" the valley asks. "Asleep?" the whole night wants to know. The sound fills all space. We scramble to our feet and stand erect in perfect confidence. They have not touched their guns.

I stand imagining them on their side of the valley as they listen, hear, receive this human voice, this voice that obviously has not stirred them to anger since no finger has pressed a trigger. True, they do not answer, they are silent; but how attentive must be that silent audience from which, a moment ago, a match had sufficed to draw a volley. Borne on the breeze of a human voice, invisible seeds are fertilizing that black earth across the valley. Those men thirst for our words as we for theirs. But their fingers, meanwhile, are on their triggers. They put me in mind of those wild things we would try in the desert to tame and that would stare at us, eat the food and drink the water we set out for them, and would spring at our throats when we made a move to stroke them.

We squatted well down behind the wall and held up a lighted match above it. Three bullets passed overhead. To the match they said, "You are forgetting that we are at war." To us, "We are listening, nevertheless. We can still love, though we stick to our rules."

Another giant peasant rested his gun against the wall, stood up, drew a deep breath, and let go:

"Antonio . . . o! It's me! Leo!"

The sound moved across the valley like a ship new-launched. Eight hundred yards to the far shore, eight hundred back—sixteen hundred yards. If they answered, there would be five seconds of time between our questions and their replies. Five seconds of silence, in which all war would be suspended, would go by between each question and each answer. Like an embassy on a journey, each time. What this meant was that even if they answered, we should still feel ourselves separated from them. Between them and us the inertia of an invisible world would still be there to be stirred into action. For the considerable space of five seconds we should be like men shipwrecked and fearful lest the rescue party had not heard their cries.

". . . ooo!"

A distant voice like a feeble wave has curled up to die on our shore. The phrase, the word, was lost on the way and the result is an undecipherable message. Yet it strikes me like a blow. In this impenetrable darkness a sudden flash of light has gleamed. All of us are shaken by a ridiculous hope. Something has made known to us its existence. We can be sure now that there are men across the way. It is as if in invisibility a crack had opened, as if . . . Imagine a house at night, dark and its doors all locked. You, sitting in its darkness, suddenly feel a breath of cold air on your face. A single breath. What a presence!

There it comes again! ". . . time . . . sleep!"

Torn, mutilated as a truly urgent message must be, washed by the waves and soaked in brine, here is our message. The men who fired at our cigarettes have blown up their chests with air in order to send us this motherly bit of advice:

"Quiet! Go to bed! Time to sleep!"

It excites us. You who read this will perhaps think that these men were merely playing a game. In a sense they were. I am sure that, being simple men, if you had caught them at their sport they would have denied that it was serious. But games always cover something deep and intense, else there would be no excitement in them, no pleasure, no power to stir us. Here was a game that made our hearts beat too wildly not to satisfy a real though undefined need within us. It was as if we were marrying our enemy before dying of his blow.

But so slight, so fragile was the pontoon flung between our two shores that a question too awkward, a phrase too clumsy, would certainly upset it. Words lose themselves: only essential words, only the truth of truths would leave this frail bridge whole. And I can see him now, that peasant who stirred Antonio to speech and thus made himself our pilot, our ambassador; I can see him as he stood erect, as he rested his strong hands on the low stone wall and sent forth from his great chest that question of questions:

"Antonio! What are you fighting for?"

Let me say again that he and Antonio would be ashamed to think that you took them seriously. They would insist that it was all in fun. But I was there as he stood waiting, and I know that his whole soul gaped wide to receive the answer. Here is the truncated message, the secret mutilated by five seconds of travel across the valley as an inscription in stone is defaced by the passing of the centuries:

"... Spain!"

And then I heard:

"... You?"

He got his answer. I heard the great reply as it was flung forth into space:

"The bread of our brothers!"

And then the amazing:

"Good night, friend!"

And the response from the other side of the world:

"Good night, friend!"

And silence.

Their words were not the same, but their truths were identical. Why has this high communion never yet prevented men from dying in battle against each other?

V

Back on the Madrid front I sat again at night in a subterranean chamber, at supper with a young captain and a few of his men. The telephone had rung and the captain was being ordered to prepare to attack before daybreak. Twenty houses in this industrial suburb, Carabanchel, constituted the objective. There would be no support: one after the other the houses were to be blown in with hand grenades and occupied.

I felt vaguely squeamish as I took something like a last look at these men who were shortly to dive into the great bowl of air, suck the blue night into their lungs, and then be blown to bits before they could reach the other side of the road. They were taking it easily enough, but the captain came back to table from the telephone shrugging his shoulders. "The first man out . . ." He started to say something, changed his mind, pushed two glasses and a bottle of brandy across the table, and said to the sergeant:

"You lead the file with me. Have a drink and go get some sleep."

The sergeant drank and went off to sleep. Round the table a dozen of us were sitting up. All the chinks in this room were caulked up; not a trickle of light could escape; the glare within was so dazzling that I blinked. The brandy was sweet, faintly nauseating, and its taste was as mournful as a drizzle at daybreak. I was in a daze, and when I had drunk I shut my eyes and saw behind my lids those ruined and ghostly houses bathed in a greenish radiance as of moonglow under water, that I had stared at a few minutes before through the sentry's loophole. Someone on my right was telling a funny story. He was talking very fast and I understood about one word in three.

A man came in half drunk, reeling gently in this half-real world. He stood rubbing a stubble of beard and looking us over with vague affectionate eyes. His glance slid across to the bottle, avoided it, came back to it, and turned pleadingly to the captain.

The captain laughed softly, and the man, suddenly hopeful, laughed too. A light gust of laughter ran over the roomful of men. The captain put out his hand and moved the bottle noiselessly out of reach. The man's glance simulated despair, and a childish game began, a sort of mute ballet which, in the fog of cigarette smoke and the weariness of the watch with its anticipation of the coming attack, was utterly dream-like. I sat hypnotized by this atmosphere of the slowly ending vigil, reading the hour in the stubbles of beard while out of doors a sea-like pounding of cannon waxed in intensity.

Soon afterwards these men were to scour themselves clean of their sweat, their brandy, the filth of their vigil, in the regal waters of the night of war. I felt in them something so near to spotless purity! Meanwhile, as long as it would last, they were dancing the ballet of the drunkard and the bottle. They were determined that this game should absorb them utterly. They were making life last as long as it possibly could. But there on a shelf stood a battered alarm clock, set to sound the zero-hour. No one so much as glanced at it but me, and my glance was furtive. They would all hear it well enough, never fear! Its ringing would shatter the stifling air.

The clock would ring out. The men would rise to their feet and stretch themselves. They would be sure to make this gesture which is instinctive in every man about to tackle the problem of survival. They would stretch themselves, I say, and they would buckle on their harness. The captain would pull his revolver out of his holster. The drunk would sober up. And all these men, without undue haste, would file into the passage. They would go as far as that rectangle of pale light which is the sky at the end of the passage, and there they would mutter something simple like "Look at that moon!" or "What a night!" And then they would fling themselves into the stars.

Scarcely had the attack been called off by telephone, scarcely had these men, most of whom had been doomed to die in the attack upon that concrete wall, begun to feel themselves safe, begun to realize that they were certain of trampling their sweet planet in their rough clogs one more day, scarcely were their minds at peace, when all in chorus began to lament their fate.

"Do they think we are a lot of women?" "Is this a war or isn't it?" A fine general staff! they grumbled sarcastically. Can't make up its mind about anything! Wants to see Madrid bombarded and kids smashed to bits. Here they were, ready to rip up those enemy batteries and fling them over the backs of mountains to save innocence imperiled, and the staff tied them hand and foot, condemned them to inaction.

It was clear enough, and the men admitted it, that none of them might have come up again after their dive

into the moonlight, and that they ought in reality to
be very happy to be alive and able to grouse against
G. H. Q. and go on drinking their consoling brandy;—
and, by the way, since the second telephone message,
two curious things had happened: the brandy tasted better and the men were now drinking it cheerfully instead
of moodily.

Yet at the same time I saw nothing in their vehemence
that made me think it either silly or boastful. I could
not but remember that all of them had been ready to
die with simplicity.

Day broke. I scrubbed my face in the freezing water
of the village pump. Coffee steamed in the bowls under
an arbor forty yards from the enemy outpost, half-
wrecked by the midnight firing but safe in the truce of
dawn. Now freshly washed, the survivors gathered
here to commune in life rather than in death, to share
their white bread, their cigarettes, their smiles. They
came in one by one, the captain, Sergeant R——, the
lieutenant, and the rest, planted their elbows solidly on
the table, and sat facing this treasure which they had
been judicious enough to despise at a moment when it
seemed it must be abandoned, but which had now re-
covered its price. "*Salud, amigo!*"—"Hail, friend!"—
they sang out as they clapped one another on the
shoulder.

I loved the freezing wind that caressed us and the

shining sun that warmed us beneath the touch of the wind. I loved the mountain air that was filling me with gladness. I rejoiced in the cheer of these men who sat in their shirtsleeves gathering fresh strength from their repast and making ready, once they had finished and risen to their feet, to knead the stuff of the world.

A ripe pod burst somewhere. From time to time a silly bullet spat against the stone wall. Death was abroad, of course, but wandering aimlessly and without ill intent. This was not death's hour. We in the arbor were celebrating life.

This whole platoon had risen up *de profundis;* and the captain sat breaking the white bread, that densely baked bread of Spain so rich in wheat, in order that each of his comrades, having stretched forth his hand, might receive a chunk as big as his fist and turn it into life.

These men had in truth risen *de profundis*. They were in very fact beginning a new life. I stared at them, and in particular at Sergeant R——, he who was to have been the first man out and who had gone to sleep in preparation for the attack. I was with them when they woke him up. Now Sergeant R—— had been well aware that he was to be the first man to step out into the line of fire of a machine-gun nest and dance in the moonlight that brief ballet at the end of which is death. His awakening had been the awakening of a prisoner in the death cell.

At Carabanchel the trenches wound among little workmen's houses whose furnishings were still in place. In one of these, a few yards from the enemy, Sergeant R—— was sleeping fully dressed on an iron cot. When we had lighted a candle and had stuck it into the neck of a bottle, and had drawn forth out of the darkness that funereal bed, the first thing that came into view was a pair of clogs. Enormous clogs, iron-shod and studded with nails, the clogs of a sewer-worker or a railway trackwalker. All the poverty of the world was in those clogs. No man ever strode with happy steps through life in clogs like these: he boarded life like a longshoreman for whom life is a ship to be unloaded.

This man was shod in his tools, and his whole body was covered with the tools of his trade—cartridge belt, gun, leather harness. His neck was bent beneath the heavy collar of the draught horse. Deep in caves, in Morocco, you can see millstones worked by blind horses. Here in the ruddy wavering light of the candle we were waking up a blind horse and sending him out to the mill.

"Hi! Sergeant!"

He sent forth a sigh as heavy as a wave and turned slowly and massively over towards us so that we saw a face still asleep and filled with anguish. His eyes were shut, and his mouth, to which clung a bubble of air, was half open like the mouth of a drowned man. We sat down on his bed and watched his laborious awakening. The man was clinging like a crab to submarine depths, grasping in his fists I know not what dark sea-weed. He opened and shut his hands, pulled up another deep sigh, and escaped from us suddenly with his face to the wall, obstinate with the stubbornness of an animal refusing to die, turning its back on the slaughter-house.

"Hi! Sergeant!"

Once again he was drawn up from the bottom of the sea, swam towards us, and we saw again his face in the candle-light. This time we had hobbled our sleeper; he would not get away from us again. He blinked with closed eyes, moved his mouth round as if swallowing, ran his hand over his forehead, made one great effort to sink back into his happy dreams and reject our universe of dynamite, weariness, and glacial night, but it was too late. Something from without was too strong for him.

Like the punished schoolboy stirred by the insistent bell out of his dream of a school-less world, Sergeant R—— began to clothe himself in the weary flesh he had so recently shed, that flesh which in the chill of awakening was soon to know the old pains in the joints, the weight of the harness, and the stumbling race towards death. Not so much death as the discomfort of dying, the filth of the blood in which he would steep his hands when he tried to rise to his feet; the stickiness of that coagulating syrup. Not so much death as the Calvary of a punished child.

One by one he stretched his arms and then his legs, bringing up an elbow, straightening a knee, while his straps, his gun, his cartridge belt, the three grenades hanging from his belt, all hampered the final strokes of this swimmer in the sea of sleep. At last he opened his eyes, sat up on the bed, and stared at us, mumbling:

"Huh! Oh! Are we off?"

And as he spoke, he simply stretched out his hand for his rifle.

"No," said the captain. "The attack has been called off."

Sergeant R——, let me tell you that we made you a present of your life. Just that. As much as if you had stood at the foot of the electric chair. And God knows, the world sheds ink enough on the pathos of pardon at the foot of the electric chair. We brought you your pardon *in extremis*. No question about it. In your mind there was nothing between you and death but a thickness of tissue-paper. Therefore you must forgive me my curiosity. I stared at you, and I shall never forget your face. It was a face touching and ugly, with a humped nose a little too big, high cheek-bones, and the spectacles of an intellectual. How does a man receive the gift of life? I can answer that. A man sits still, pulls a bit of tobacco out of his pocket, nods his head slowly, looks up at the ceiling, and says:

"Suits me."

Then he nods his head again and adds:

"If they'd sent us a couple of platoons the attack might have made sense. The lads would have pitched in. You'd have seen what they can do."

Sergeant, Sergeant, what will you do with this gift of life?

Now, Sergeant at peace, you are dipping your bread into your coffee. You are rolling cigarettes. You are like the lad who has been told he will not be punished after all. And yet, like the rest, you are ready to start out again tonight on that brief dash at the end of which the only thing a man can do is kneel down.

Over and over in my head there goes the question I have wanted to ask you ever since last night: "Sergeant, what is it makes you willing to die?"

But I know that it is impossible to ask such a question. It would offend a modesty in you which you yourself do not know to be there, but which would never forgive me. You could not answer with high-sounding words: they would seem false to you and in truth they would be false. What language could be chaste enough for a modest man like you? But I am determined to know, and I shall try to get round the difficulty. I shall ask you seemingly idle questions, and you will answer.

"Tell me, why did you join up?"

If I understood your answer, Sergeant, you hardly know yourself. You were a bookkeeper in Barcelona. You added up your columns of figures every day without worrying much about the struggle against the rebels. But one of your friends joined up, and then a second friend; and you were disturbed to find yourself undergoing a curious transformation: little by little your columns of figures seemed to you futile. Your pleasures, your work, your dreams, all seemed to belong to another age.

But even that was not important, until one day you heard that one of your friends had been killed on the Málaga front. He was not a friend for whom you would ever have felt you had to lay down your life. Yet that bit of news swept over you, over your narrow little life, like a wind from the sea. And that morning another friend had looked at you and said, "Do we or don't we?" And you had said, "We do."

You never really wondered about the imperious call that compelled you to join up. You accepted a truth which you could never translate into words, but whose self-evidence overpowered you. And while I sat listening to your story, an image came into my mind, and I understood.

When the wild ducks or the wild geese migrate in their season, a strange tide rises in the territories over which they sweep. As if magnetized by the great triangular flight, the barnyard fowl leap a foot or two into the air and try to fly. The call of the wild strikes them with the force of a harpoon and a vestige of savagery quickens their blood. All the ducks on the farm are transformed for an instant into migrant birds, and into those hard little heads, till now filled with humble images of pools and worms and barnyards, there swims a sense of continental expanse, of the breadth of seas and the salt taste of the ocean wind. The duck totters to right and left in its wire enclosure, gripped by a sudden passion to perform the impossible and a sudden love whose object is a mystery.

Even so is man overwhelmed by a mysterious presentiment of truth, so that he discovers the vanity of his bookkeeping and the emptiness of his domestic felicities. But he can never put a name to this sovereign truth. Men explain these brusque vocations by the need to escape or the lure of danger, as if we knew where the need to escape and the lure of danger themselves came from. They talk about the call of duty, but what is it that makes the call of duty so pressing? What can you tell me, Sergeant, about that uneasiness that seeped in to disturb your peaceful existence?

The call that stirred you must torment all men. Whether we dub it sacrifice, or poetry, or adventure, it is always the same voice that calls. But domestic security has succeeded in crushing out that part in us that is capable of heeding the call. We scarcely quiver; we beat our wings once or twice and fall back into our barnyard.

We are prudent people. We are afraid to let go of our petty reality in order to grasp at a great shadow. But you, Sergeant, did discover the sordidness of those shop-keepers' bustlings, those petty pleasures, those petty needs. You felt that men did not live like this. And you agreed to heed the great call without bothering to try to understand it. The hour had come when you must moult, when you must rise into the sky.

The barnyard duck had no notion that his little head was big enough to contain oceans, continents, skies; but of a sudden here he was beating his wings, despising corn, despising worms, battling to become a wild duck.

There is a day of the year when the eels must go down to the Sargasso Sea, and come what may, no one can prevent them. On that day they spit upon their ease, their tranquillity, their tepid waters. Off they go over ploughed fields, pricked by the hedges and skinned by the stones, in search of the river that leads to the abyss.

Even so did you feel yourself swept away by that inward migration about which no one had ever said a word to you. You were ready for a sort of bridal that was a mystery to you, but in which you had to partici-pate. "Do we or don't we? We do." You went up to the front in a war that at bottom meant little to you. You took to the road as spontaneously as that silvery people shining in the fields on its way to the sea, or that black triangle in the sky.

What were you after? Last night you almost reached your goal. What was it you discovered in yourself that was so ready to burst from its cocoon? At daybreak your comrades were full of complaint: tell me, of what had they been defrauded? What had they discovered in themselves that was about to show itself, and that now they wept for?

What, Sergeant, were the visions that governed your destiny and justified your risking your life in this adventure? Your life, your only treasure! We have to live a long time before we become men. Very slowly do we plait the braid of friendships and affections. We learn slowly. We compose our creation slowly. And if we die too early we are in a sense cheated out of our share. We have to live a long time to fulfil ourselves.

But you, by the grace of an ordeal in the night which stripped you of all that was not intrinsic, you discovered a mysterious creature born of yourself. Great was this creature, and never shall you forget him. And he is yourself. You have had the sudden sense of fulfilling yourself in the instant of discovery, and you have learned suddenly that the future is now less necessary for the accumulation of treasures. That creature within you who opened his wings is not bound by ties to perishable things; he agrees to die for all men, to be swallowed up in something universal.

A great wind swept through you and delivered from the matrix the sleeping prince you sheltered—Man within you. You are the equal of the musician composing his music, of the physicist extending the frontier of knowledge, of all those who build the highways over which we march to deliverance. Now you are free to gamble with death. What have you now to lose?

Let us say you were happy in Barcelona: nothing more can ruin that happiness. You have reached an altitude where all loves are of the same stuff. Perhaps you suffered on earth, felt yourself alone on the planet, knew no refuge to which you might fly? What of that! Sergeant, this day you have been welcomed home by love.

VI

No man can draw a free breath who does not share with other men a common and disinterested ideal. Life has taught us that love does not consist in gazing at each other but in looking outward together in the same direction. There is no comradeship except through union in the same high effort. Even in our age of material well-being this must be so, else how should we explain the happiness we feel in sharing our last crust with others in the desert? No sociologist's textbook can prevail against this fact. Every pilot who has flown to the rescue of a comrade in distress knows that all joys are vain in comparison with this one. And this, it may be, is the reason why the world today is tumbling about our ears. It is precisely because this sort of fulfilment is promised each of us by his religion, that men are inflamed today. All of us, in words that contradict each other, express at bottom the same exalted impulse. What sets us against one another is not our aims—they all come to the same thing —but our methods, which are the fruit of our varied reasoning.

Let us, then, refrain from astonishment at what men do. One man finds that his essential manhood comes alive at the sight of self-sacrifice, cooperative effort, a rigorous vision of justice, manifested in an anarchists' cellar in Barcelona. For that man there will henceforth be but one truth—the truth of the anarchists. Another, having once mounted guard over a flock of terrified little nuns kneeling in a Spanish nunnery, will thereafter know a different truth—that it is sweet to die for the Church. If, when Mermoz plunged into the Chilean Andes with victory in his heart, you had protested to him that no merchant's letter could possibly be worth risking one's life for, Mermoz would have laughed in your face. Truth is the man that was born in Mermoz when he slipped through the Andean passes.

Consider that officer of the South Moroccan Rifles who, during the war in the Rif, was in command of an outpost set down between two mountains filled with enemy tribesmen. One day, down from the mountain to the west came a group seeking a parley. Arabs and Frenchmen were talking over their tea when of a sudden a volley rang out. The tribesmen from the other mountain were charging the post. When the commandant sought to dismiss his guests before fighting off their allies, they said to him: "Today we are your guests. God will not allow us to desert you." They fought beside his men, saved the post, and then climbed back into their eyrie.

But on the eve of the day when their turn had come to pounce upon the post they sent again to the commandant.

"We came to your aid the other day," their chief said.

"True."

"We used up three hundred of our cartridges for you."

"Very likely."

"It would be only just that you replace them for us."

The commandant was an officer and a gentleman. They were given their cartridges.

Truth, for any man, is that which makes him a man. A man who has fraternized with men on this high plane, who has displayed this sportsmanship and has seen the rules of the game so nobly observed on both sides in matters of life and death, is obviously not to be mentioned in the same breath with the shabby hearty demagogue who would have expressed his fraternity with the Arabs by a great clap on the shoulders and a spate of flattering words that would have humiliated them. You might argue with the captain that all was fair in war, but if you did he would feel a certain pitying contempt for you. And he would be right.

Meanwhile, you are equally right to hate war.

If our purpose is to understand mankind and its yearnings, to grasp the essential reality of mankind, we must never set one man's truth against another's. All beliefs are demonstrably true. All men are demonstrably in the right. Anything can be demonstrated by logic. I say that that man is right who blames all the ills of the world upon hunchbacks. Let us declare war on hunchbacks—and in the twinkling of an eye all of us will hate them fanatically. All of us will join to avenge the crimes of the hunchbacks. Assuredly, hunchbacks, too, do commit crimes.

But if we are to succeed in grasping what is essential in man, we must put aside the passions that divide us and that, once they are accepted, sow in the wind a whole Koran of unassailable verities and fanaticisms. Nothing is easier than to divide men into rightists and leftists, hunchbacks and straightbacks, fascists and democrats—and these distinctions will be perfectly just. But truth, we know, is that which clarifies, not that which confuses. Truth is the language that expresses universality. Newton did not "discover" a law that lay hidden from man like the answer to a rebus. He accomplished a creative operation. He founded a human speech which could express at one and the same time the fall of an apple and the rising of the sun. Truth is not that which is demonstrable but that which is ineluctable.

There is no profit in discussing ideologies. If all of them are logically demonstrable then all of them must

contradict one other. To agree to discuss them is tanta-
mount to despairing of the salvation of mankind—
whereas everywhere about us men manifest identical
yearnings.

What all of us want is to be set free. The man who
sinks his pickaxe into the ground wants that stroke to
mean something. The convict's stroke is not the same as
the prospector's, for the obvious reason that the prospector's stroke has meaning and the convict's stroke has
none. It would be a mistake to think that the prison exists at the point where the convict's stroke is dealt.
Prison is not a mere physical horror. It is using a pickaxe
to no purpose that makes a prison; the horror resides in
the failure to enlist all those who swing the pick in the
community of mankind.

We all yearn to escape from prison.

There are two hundred million men in Europe whose
existence has no meaning and who yearn to come alive.
Industry has torn them from the idiom of their peasant lineage and has locked them up in those enormous
ghettos that are like railway yards heaped with blackened trucks. Out of the depths of their slums these
men yearn to be awakened. There are others, caught
in the wheels of a thousand trades, who are forbidden
to share in the joys known to a Mermoz, to a priest,
to a man of science. Once it was believed that to
bring these creatures to manhood it was enough to feed

them, clothe them, and look to their everyday needs; but we see now that the result of this has been to turn out petty shopkeepers, village politicians, hollow technicians devoid of an inner life. Some indeed were well taught, but no one troubled to cultivate any of them. People who believe that culture consists in the capacity to remember formulae have a paltry notion of what it is. Of course any science student can tell us more about Nature and her laws than can Descartes or Newton,— but what can he tell us about the human spirit?

With more or less awareness, all men feel the need to come alive. But most of the methods suggested for bringing this about are snares and delusions. Men can of course be stirred into life by being dressed up in uniforms and made to blare out chants of war. It must be confessed that this is one way for men to break bread with comrades and to find what they are seeking, which is a sense of something universal, of self-fulfilment. But of this bread men die.

It is easy to dig up wooden idols and revive ancient and more or less workable myths like Pan-Germanism or the Roman Empire. The Germans can intoxicate themselves with the intoxication of being Germans and compatriots of Beethoven. A stoker in the hold of a freighter can be made drunk with this drink. What is more difficult is to bring up a Beethoven out of the stoke-hold.

These idols, in sum, are carnivorous idols. The man

who dies for the progress of science or the healing of the sick serves life in his very dying. It may be glorious to die for the expansion of territory, but modern warfare destroys what it claims to foster. The day is gone when men sent life coursing through the veins of a race by the sacrifice of a little blood. War carried on by gas and bombing is no longer war, it is a kind of bloody surgery. Each side settles down behind a concrete wall and finds nothing better to do than to send forth, night after night, squadrons of planes to bomb the guts of the other side, blow up its factories, paralyze its production, and abolish its trade. Such a war is won by him who rots last —but in the end both rot together.

In a world become a desert we thirst for comradeship. It is the savor of bread broken with comrades that makes us accept the values of war. But there are other ways than war to bring us the warmth of a race, shoulder to shoulder, towards an identical goal. War has tricked us. It is not true that hatred adds anything to the exaltation of the race.

Why should we hate one another? We all live in the same cause, are borne through life on the same planet, form the crew of the same ship. Civilizations may, indeed, compete to bring forth new syntheses, but it is monstrous that they should devour one another.

To set man free it is enough that we help one another to realize that there does exist a goal towards which all mankind is striving. Why should we not strive towards that goal together, since it is what unites us all? The surgeon pays no heed to the moanings of his patient: beyond that pain it is man he is seeking to heal. That surgeon speaks a universal language. The physicist does the same when he ponders those almost divine equations in which he seizes the whole physical universe from the atom to the nebula. Even the simple shepherd modestly watching his sheep under the stars would discover, once he understood the part he was playing, that he was something more than a servant, was a sentinel. And each sentinel among men is responsible for the whole of the empire.

It is impossible not to believe that the shepherd wants to understand. One day, on the Madrid front, I chanced upon a school that stood on a hill surrounded by a low stone wall some five hundred yards behind the trenches. A corporal was teaching botany that day. He was lecturing on the fragile organs of a poppy held in his hands. Out of the surrounding mud, and in spite of the wandering shells that dropped all about, he had drawn like a magnet an audience of stubble-bearded soldiers who squatted tailor fashion and listened with their chins in their hands to a discourse of which they understood not a word in five. Something within them had said: "You are but brutes fresh from your caves. Go along! Catch up with humanity!" And they had hurried on their muddy clogs to overtake it.

It is only when we become conscious of our part in life, however modest, that we shall be happy. Only then will we be able to live in peace and die in peace, for only this lends meaning to life and to death.

Death is sweet when it comes in its time and in its place, when it is part of the order of things, when the old peasant of Provence, at the end of his reign, remits into the hands of his sons his parcel of goats and olive-trees in order that they in their turn transmit them to their sons. When one is part of a peasant lineage, one's death is only half a death. Each life in turn bursts like a pod and sends forth its seed.

I stood once with three peasants in the presence of their dead mother. Sorrow filled the room. For a second time, the umbilical cord had been cut. For a second time the knot had been loosed, the knot that bound one generation to another. Of a sudden the three sons had felt themselves alone on earth with everything still to be learned. The magnetic pole round which they had lived was gone; their mother's table, where they had collected on feast days with their families, was no more. But I could see in this rupture that it was possible for life to be granted a second time. Each of these sons was now to be the head of a family, was to be a rallying point and a patriarch, until that day when each would pass on the staff of office to the brood of children now murmuring in the courtyard.

I looked at their mother, at the old peasant with the firm peaceful face, the tight lips, the human face transformed into a stone mask. I saw in it the faces of her sons. That mask had served to mould theirs. That body had served to mould the bodies of these three exemplary men who stood there as upright as trees. And now she lay broken but at rest, a vein from which the gold had been extracted. In their turn, her sons and daughters would bring forth men from their mould. One does not die on a farm: their mother is dead, long live their mother!

Sorrowful, yes, but so simple was this image of a lineage dropping one by one its white-haired members as it made its way through time and through its metamorphoses towards a truth that was its own.

That same day, when the tocsin tolled to announce to the countryside the death of this old woman, it seemed to me not a song of despair but a discreet and tender chant of joy. In that same voice the church-bell celebrated birth and death, christening and burial, the passage from one generation to the next. I was suffused with a gentle peace of soul at this sound which announced the betrothal of a poor old woman and the earth.

This was life that was handed on here from generation to generation with the slow progress of a tree's growth, but it was also fulfilment. What a mysterious ascension! From a little bubbling lava, from the vague pulp of a star, from a living cell miraculously fertilized, we have issued forth and have bit by bit raised ourselves to the writing of cantatas and the weighing of nebulae.

This peasant mother had done more than transmit life, she had taught her sons a language, had handed on to them the lot so slowly garnered through the centuries, the spiritual patrimony of traditions, concepts, and myths that make up the whole of the difference between Newton or Shakespeare and the caveman.

What we feel when we are hungry, when we feel that hunger which drew the Spanish soldiers under fire towards that botany lesson, drew Mermoz across the South Atlantic, draws a man to a poem, is that the birth of man is not yet accomplished, that we must take stock of ourselves and our universe. We must send forth pontoons into the night. There are men unaware of this, imagining themselves wise and self-regarding because they are indifferent. But everything in the world gives the lie to their wisdom.

Comrades of the air! I call upon you to bear me witness. When have we felt ourselves happy men?

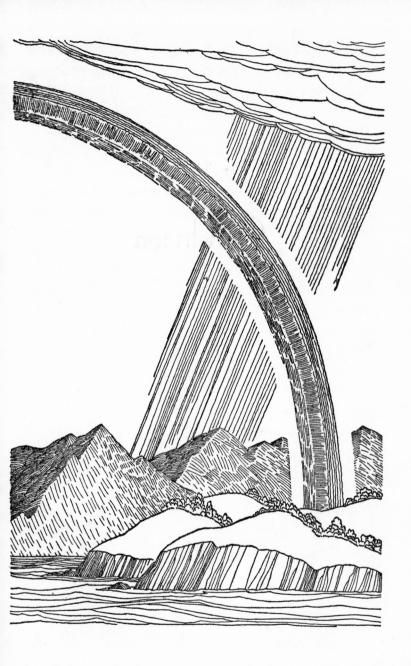

· 10 ·

Conclusion

H ERE, in the final pages of this book, I remember again those musty civil servants who served as our escort in the omnibus when we set out to fly our first mails, when we prepared ourselves to be transformed into men—we who had had the luck to be called. Those clerks were kneaded of the same stuff as the rest of us, but they knew not that they were hungry.

To come to man's estate it is not necessary to get oneself killed round Madrid, or to fly mail planes, or to struggle wearily in the snows out of respect for the dignity of life. The man who can see the miraculous in a poem, who can take pure joy from music, who can break his bread with comrades, opens his window to the same refreshing wind off the sea. He too learns a language of men.

But too many men are left unawakened.

A few years ago, in the course of a long railway journey, I was suddenly seized by a desire to make a tour of the little country in which I was locked up for three days, cradled in that rattle that is like the sound of pebbles rolled over and over by the waves; and I got up out of my berth. At one in the morning I went through the train in all its length. The sleeping cars were empty. The first-class carriages were empty. They put me in mind of the luxurious hotels on the Riviera that open in winter for a single guest, the last representative of an extinct fauna. A sign of bitter times.

But the third-class carriages were crowded with hundreds of Polish workmen sent home from France. I made my way along those passages, stepping over sprawling bodies and peering into the carriages. In the dim glow cast by the night-lamps into these barren and comfortless compartments I saw a confused mass of people churned about by the swaying of the train, the whole thing looking and smelling like a barrack-room. A whole nation returning to its native poverty seemed to sprawl there in a sea of bad dreams. Great shaven heads rolled on the cushionless benches. Men, women, and children were stirring in their sleep, tossing from left to right and back again as if attacked by all the noises and jerkings that threatened them in their oblivion. They had not found the hospitality of a sweet slumber.

Looking at them I said to myself that they had lost half their human quality. These people had been knocked about from one end of Europe to the other by the economic currents; they had been torn from their little houses in the north of France, from their tiny garden-plots, their three pots of geranium that always stood in the windows of the Polish miners' families. I saw lying beside them pots and pans, blankets, curtains, bound into bundles badly tied and swollen with hernias.

Out of all that they had caressed or loved in France, out of everything they had succeeded in taming in their four or five years in my country—the cat, the dog, the geranium—they had been able to bring away with them only a few kitchen utensils, two or three blankets, a curtain or so.

A baby lay at the breast of a mother so weary that she seemed asleep. Life was being transmitted in the shabbiness and the disorder of this journey. I looked at the father. A powerful skull as naked as a stone. A body hunched over in uncomfortable sleep, imprisoned in working clothes, all humps and hollows. The man looked like a lump of clay, like one of those sluggish and shape-less derelicts that crumple into sleep in our public markets.

And I thought: The problem does not reside in this

poverty, in this filth, in this ugliness. But this same man and this same woman met one day. This man must have smiled at this woman. He may, after his work was done, have brought her flowers. Timid and awkward, perhaps he trembled lest she disdain him. And this woman, out of natural coquetry, this woman sure of her charms, perhaps took pleasure in teasing him. And this man, this man who is now no more than a machine for swinging a pick or a sledge-hammer, must have felt in his heart a delicious anguish. The mystery is that they should have become these lumps of clay. Into what terrible mould were they forced? What was it that marked them like this as if they had been put through a monstrous stamping machine? A deer, a gazelle, any animal grown old, preserves its grace. What is it that corrupts this wonderful clay of which man is kneaded?

I went on through these people whose slumber was as sinister as a den of evil. A vague noise floated in the air made up of raucous snores, obscure moanings, and the scraping of clogs as their wearers, broken on one side, sought comfort on the other. And always the muted accompaniment of those pebbles rolled over and over by the waves.

I sat down face to face with one couple. Between the man and the woman a child had hollowed himself out a place and fallen asleep. He turned in his slumber, and in the dim lamplight I saw his face. What an adorable face!

A golden fruit had been born of these two peasants. Forth from this sluggish scum had sprung this miracle of delight and grace.

I bent over the smooth brow, over those mildly pouting lips, and I said to myself: This is a musician's face. This is the child Mozart. This is a life full of beautiful promise. Little princes in legends are not different from this. Protected, sheltered, cultivated, what could not this child become?

When by mutation a new rose is born in a garden, all the gardeners rejoice. They isolate the rose, tend it, foster it. But there is no gardener for men. This little Mozart will be shaped like the rest by the common stamping machine. This little Mozart will love shoddy music in the stench of night dives. This little Mozart is condemned.

I went back to my sleeping car. I said to myself: Their fate causes these people no suffering. It is not an impulse to charity that has upset me like this. I am not weeping over an eternally open wound. Those who carry the wound do not feel it. It is the human race and not the individual that is wounded here, is outraged here. I do not believe in pity. What torments me tonight is the gardener's point of view. What torments me is not this poverty to which after all a man can accustom himself as easily as to sloth. Generations of Orientals live in filth and love it. What torments me is not the humps nor the hollows nor the ugliness. It is the sight, a little bit in all these men, of Mozart murdered.

Only the Spirit, if it breathe upon the clay, can create Man.

THE END